AFRICA.com

AFRICA.com

Digital, Economic, Cultural Transformations

Jean-Louis Roy

In Collaboration with
Solim Baba Pekele

Translated by Jonathan Burnham

Library and Archives Canada Cataloguing in Publication

Title: Africa.com: digital, economic, cultural transformations / Jean-Louis Roy.

Other titles: Bienvenue en Afrique. English

Names: Roy, Jean-Louis, 1941- author.

Description: Translation of: Bienvenue en Afrique.

Identifiers: Canadiana (print) 20210135506
Canadiana (ebook) 20210138580

ISBN 9781771615563 (softcover) ISBN 9781771615570 (PDF)
ISBN 9781771615587 (EPUB) ISBN 9781771615594 (Kindle)

Subjects: LCSH: Economic development—Africa. | LCSH: Africa—Economic conditions. | LCSH: Africa—Foreign economic relations—Asia. | LCSH: Asia—Foreign economic relations—Africa.

Classification: LCC HC800 .R68813 2021
DDC 338.90096—dc23

Published by Mosaic Press, Oakville, Ontario, Canada, 2021.

MOSAIC PRESS, Publishers
www.Mosaic-Press.com

Printed and bound in Canada.

Cover Design by Brianna Wodabek

Funded by the Government of Canada
Financé par le gouvernement du Canada

MOSAIC PRESS
1252 Speers Road, Units 1 & 2, Oakville, Ontario, L6L 5N9
(905) 825-2130 • info@mosaic-press.com • www.mosaic-press.com

CONTENTS

Introduction 1

Chapter One:

Global Transformations and Africa 13

Chapter Two:

Creating Wealth by and for Africans 40

Chapter Three:

Areas for Growth Potential 87

Conclusions 105

Bibliography 113

List of Acronyms

AAIA African Automotive Industry Alliance
ADB African Development Bank
AGF African Guarantee Fund
AIIB Asian infrastructure Investment Bank
AUA Programme urbain pour l'Afrique
BCG Boston Consulting Group
BM Banque Mondiale
BPCE Banque Populaire et de la Caisse d'Épargne
BRVM Bourse Régionale des Valeurs Mobilières
CARIC Capacité Africaine de Réponse Immédiate aux Crises
CCCC China Communications Construction Co
CCCI Consumer Class Conditions Index
CEDEAO Communauté Économique des États de l'Afrique de l'Ouest
CEMAC Communauté Économique et Monétaire de l'Afrique Centrale
CGLUA Organisation des Cités et gouvernements locaux Unis d'Afrique
CHEC China Harbour Engineering Company
CICA Chambre Internationale de Commerce Africain
CIPESA Collaboration on International ICT Policy in East and Southern Africa
CMA-CGM Compagnie Maritime d'Affrètement — Compagnie Générale Maritime

CMEC Chinese Machinery Engineering Corporation
COMESA Marché commun des États de l'Afrique australe et de l'Est
COP22 22nd Conference of the Parties, held in Marrakech in 2016
EAC Communauté de l'Afrique de l'Est
EPA Economic Partnership Agreements
FAA Force Africaine en Attente
FAGACE Fonds Africain de Garantie et de Coopération Économique
FCFA Franc de la Communauté Française Africaine
FIBA Fédération Internationale de Basketball
FMI Fonds Monétaire International
FOCAC Forum sur la coopération sino-africaine
FSA Fonds de Solidarité Africain
GHIT The Global Innovative Technology Fund
GSMA Association internationale d'opérateurs de téléphonie mobile
IATA International Air Transport Association
IPCC Intergovernmental Panel on Climate Change
JSE Bourse de Johannesburg
MBA Ligue nationale de basketball américaine
MIAF Meridian Infrastructure Africa Fund
MSC Mediterranean Shipping Company
NEPAD Nouveau partenariat pour le développement de l'Afrique
OECD Organisation for Economic Co-operation and Development
OPEC Organization of The Petroleum Exporting Countries
PAPC Pan-African Association for Port Cooperation
PMAESA Port Management Association of Eastern and Southern Africa
PMAWCA Ports Management Association of West and Central Africa
RASCOM Organisation régionale africaine de communications par satellite
SADC Communauté de développement de l'Afrique australe
SEM Stock Exchange of Mauricius
TICAD Conférence internationale de Tokyo sur le Développement de l'Afrique
ZLEC Zone de Libre-Échange Continental

Acknowledgements

This book has received the precious collaboration of many. Friendly thoughts to my African students of the Ecole Supérieure de la Francophonie pour l'Administration et le Management of Sofia, to my predictable interlocutors including my friends the Gerba, Malam and Amina. Jamal Eddine Naji, Marie-Louise Akondja, Jean-Louis Atangana, Marie-Roger Biloa, Yves Ngorbo, Dahirou Djamo, Rogatien Mante, Leinad Mvondo, Bouvy Enkobo, Christian Rodrigue Adeba, Samuel Brandson Bergsok and many others. Jean-Sébastien Bourré was my one-man proof reading committee. Ben-Marc and Bryan Diendere were privy to all my questions. Many thanks for their patience and contributions. Finally, throughout this work, I was able to count on the solid support of Solim Baba Pekele. In Lomé, this young jurist and administrator has contributed substantially to the ideation of this project, to the indispensable research and to the configuration that structure this essay. This book is his as much as it is mine.

My gratitude as well to Jonathan Burnham, who was responsible once more for making my work available to all our English-reading friends, with help from Kouakou Kouamé, in Côte d'Ivoire. Translation is so important in the publishing world and I am always happy to see my words gracefully jump the wonderful hurdle that is language. Speaking of publishers, it was really important for me to publish the French edition of this book, "Bienvenue en Afrique", in Africa. My very dear friend, Amadou Lamine Sall, so far away yet so close, once again opened wide the doors of his publishing house, *Feu de brousse* in Dakar. He, along with my poet friend Amadou Lamine Ba helped me shape the first version of the book you hold in your hands. As for this English version, my loyal friend Howard Aster at Mosaic Press has shown great interest in publishing this vision of Africa to his readers and I thank him for receiving my ideas with his unique insight and patience.

I dedicate this book to Bryan, hoping that his Africa will resemble, in the near future, the portrait we draw up in this book.

FOREWORD

The research and writing of this book were completed before the COVID-19 pandemic hit the world. Its economic effects are among the potential crises we discuss at the beginning of our second chapter, crises that could affect the dynamics at work on the continent. It could affect them, but it cannot stop them, the fundamentals of the African project being too "powerful, complementary and sustainable".

These fundamentals are the subject of this book. Their enumeration is robust and convincing: from the demographic and urban dynamics that predict a doubling of the continent's population, and of its urban population, to the conviction that Africans (2.4 billion in 2050) constitute one of the most promising markets of the century; from the new economic partnerships, particularly Asian and Arab ones, with China and the United Arab Emirates at the forefront, in addition to the traditional relations of the continent's countries. It also ranges from the spectacular growth in the volume of investment in renewable energy, land, sea, air and space transportation infrastructure to the renewal of the continent's financial institutions: banks, stock exchanges, professional associations and the spectacular rise of information technologies.

The continent had 527 million Internet users as of December 31, 2019, a growth of 11,567% since 2000. Like India and China, it should have more than a billion users in 2050. Finally, one of these fundamentals is the effective rise of a class of ambitious African entrepreneurs who see the continent as a large market in deficit of services and goods and are working to fill it, at the same time as a continental free trade area (FTAA) is gradually being built. The Moroccan companies that have established themselves throughout the continent perfectly illustrate this decisive movement.

It is likely that the COVID-19 pandemic will affect some of the fields just evoked. However, for the most part, the interests and needs of Africans and their partners will keep the current momentum. Unless there is a radical change in continental and global circumstances, the continent's development will make it the most important building site of the century and one of the engines of global growth, just as Asia has been since the juncture of the second and third millennia.

Jean-Louis Roy

INTRODUCTION

THE BUILDING SITE OF THE CENTURY

Africans are and will gradually continue to be the beneficiaries of the two mutations that are radically transforming our world: the wealth shift from the West to the East and South of the planet and the universal deployment of the digital age. The OECD has described the first as "the most important transfer in the history of mankind"[1]; the second marks the entry of the human family into a new civilization.

Situated at the heart of the DNA of history as it unfolds, these mutations affect all societies and all human beings. Their convergence has driven development in Asia over the past quarter century. From Asia, it now brings it to Africa for the benefit of Africans who have been deprived of it in the modern and contemporary period.[2] It makes Africa the building site of the century. This book tells the story of this passage, still unfinished, uneven and fluctuating depending on where you look, but robust and decisive. Here, as elsewhere in the world, demanding strategies must be adopted and implemented in order to seize this very special moment in history.

This need for strategies and their implementation is the responsibility of civil societies, private and public sector institutions and enterprises, professional corporations, universities and research centres. It is also the responsibility of national governments, as they are in charge

---

1 OECD, Perspectives on Global Development 2010, Shifting Wealth, OECD, 2010.

2 Hélène d'Almeida-Topor, « L'Afrique du 20e siècle à nos jours », Paris, Armand Colin, 2013.

of local development as well as trustees of the potential of the five African regional economic communities. Lastly, it is the responsibility of the continent in areas that require consultation and decisiveness in that regard. These strategies must bring together global mutations and those affecting all African societies.

It is announced that the continent's population could double to 2.4 billion by 2050, one billion of whom will be under 18 years old[3]. This is an increase equivalent, every ten years, to the population of the United States. The continent will then account for a quarter of humanity (25%) compared to 15% for India, 12.5% for China, 4.5% for the European Union and 4% for the United States.

It is also announced that the continent's urban population will grow spectacularly, from seven hundred and fifty million in 2030 to one billion two hundred million in 2050.

Finally, the continued expansion of its middle class, estimated today at three hundred and fifty million people, equivalent to that of China, is announced; three hundred and fifty million people today, five hundred million in 2030, and one billion in 2050. Such are the consequences of the massive capital and technology transfer, the largest in the history of mankind, to reiterate OECD's assessment.

This vast demographic enrichment, this impressive growth of cities, this rise of a middle class will all drive the demand for goods and services to continue to rise, as it has in China since the beginning of the century.

African middle-class consumption could become one of the world economy's determining levers,[4] "the lifeline of other continents", according to the assessment of Cameroonian billionaire, Baba Danpullo. A middle class whose expectations have been described by a keen observer of the continent as follows: "education, training, work, employment, accessible housing, more social justice, a possibility of modernity, or such forms of progress."[5] Perhaps also entertainment such as that which will be provided to Africans by the eventual creation of a professional basketball league involving twelve teams on the continent, sponsored by the powerful and popular National Basketball Association (NBA) and the International Basketball Federation (FIBA).

---

3 UNICEF, Generation 2030 Africa 2.0, 2017.

4 Consumption accounts for more than 50% of GDP in all the so-called developed countries and in a large number of emerging countries, including Malaysia, Mexico, Brazil, Turkey, Thailand, etc.

5 Zyad Limam, « Ambiances à Abidjan », *Afrique Magazine*, number 373, March 2018.

Is it any wonder that Africans are taking part in the current mutations of humanity, which are reaching them, and fast? Imperative, their aspirations are nourished by these multiple flows that are indeed reaching them daily and directly without the filters that, in recent centuries, have cut them off from having a direct relationship with the world. Africa's youth, as Senegalese economist Felwine Sarr rightly notes, "is characterized by a very different representation of space and narrative about its condition. It disagrees with a discourse that is projected onto it and which does not correspond to the way youth is lived elsewhere in the world". It disagrees and asks that it be left to Africans, as is the case for Asians, Europeans and all others, to decide the terms of cohabitation that bring together the universality and specificity of human experiences, both collective and individual.

Asked a thousand times, the question about the continent's take-off will continue to find its answer in the convergence between the consideration of the needs of the whole population, the requirements of this middle class, those of this youth to which are added the needs of the professional associations and the economic, financial and commercial operators of the continent, which we will get back to soon enough.

This question of the take-off of the continent will find its answer in the strong techno-economic and socio-cultural mutation in progress much more than through the work of the political class, however commendable it may be, in some cases. Indeed, change rarely comes from the political class. It is often the last stakeholder to resist, the last to espouse change, the last to give in to the needs of civil society and of the social, cultural, financial, economic and commercial operators.

This book is based on a conviction. Africa is changing at breakneck speed, as we demonstrate throughout this book. This change is now at the frontiers of politics. In several countries of the continent, these political borders have been crossed. It will be a majority of them in the foreseeable future. Politics rarely change societies, but societies often bring about political change.

In 2017, the consulting firm AT Kearney identified thirty countries in the world that would be the most promising for the distribution sector. More than a quarter of these countries are African.[6] Not surprisingly, Africans share the same common needs and hopes than most: a decent standard of living for the greatest number, a compassionate policy for the most fragile among them and a regime of

---

6 These countries are: Morocco, Algeria, Côte d'Ivoire, Tanzania, Tunisia, Kenya, South Africa and Nigeria.

rights and freedoms for all. They have learned, like their contemporaries everywhere, the value of the planet's common goods, of which they are responsible, for the most part: from the atmosphere to natural resources,[7] from biological ecosystems to the multiple functions of filiations and, foundational, the value of respecting life in its every shape or form.

These data can be broken down into multiple subsets of great importance.

Suffice it to mention that in 2050, nearly one billion people will live in the ten countries crossed by the Nile, compared to four hundred million today[8] and that there could be more than two hundred and fifty million people living in the vicinity of Lake Chad, more than double the current population. In these two cases, as in so many others, the consequences of global warming and the pressure on vital resources will be colossal; with all that being said, the need for deliberation will be imperative.

Suffice it to mention that also by the middle of the century, the majority of Africa's population will be urban and that the continent's cities will be inhabited by the world's youngest population.

Suffice it to mention that by then, Africa will be, along with India, one of the two largest emerging trading markets and one of the three largest digital communities in the world. More on that later.

Our benchmarks

Without leaving aside the traditional sources, the World Bank (WB), the International Monetary Fund (IMF), the Organization for Economic Co-operation and Development (OECD), etc., which have so powerfully contributed to structuring the narrative and the assessment of the situation of African countries in recent decades,[9] we have drawn on two other sources of information: the work of the continent's think tanks and the studies and prospective analyses of numerous international private or para-public groups interested in Africa's future.

The first of these sources consists of research and prospective analyses carried out by numerous think tanks and foundations on the continent that study "contemporary societies", to borrow the expression

---

[7] Including the inputs of 21st century energy carriers: lithium, cobalt, lead and nickel.

[8] "Food and Famine", *The Economist*, August 5, 2017.

[9] See the important publication of the French Ministry of Foreign Affairs, « Un bilan de la prospective africaine », vol. 2, 1999.

from the laboratory of the same name at the University of Yaoundé.[10] These important works are rarely referenced and cited, even though they are of high quality.

The University of Pennsylvania publishes an annual World Index of these institutions of analyses and proposals.[11] In 2017, there were 745 think tanks on the continent, 664 in sub-Saharan Africa and 81 in North Africa. They represented nearly 10% of the global total of these research and intervention groups. India and China had 293 and 512 think tanks respectively.[12]

The ongoing transformation of the continent is the focus of these groups' work. We paid attention to them throughout this book. Combining the knowledge of Africa's legacies and research on the continent's self-interests, the understanding of patrimonial and current realities, the identification of sectoral and global stakes, the studies of these African researchers constitute a formidable body of work that is insufficiently known and exploited.

Felwine Sarr[13] created, along with philosopher Achille Mbembe[14], the *Ateliers de la pensée*, held in Dakar and Saint-Louis, to think about and question contemporary Africa and the Africa of the future. In Dakar as well, Gilles Yabi set up his West African Citizen Think Tank (WATHI)[15], a veritable laboratory of ideas that seeks to shed light on the state of Africa and its inhabitants over the next five decades. Alioune Sall created the very influential African Futures Institute in Pretoria, which he directs. The former invites Africans to reflect on who they are and, more importantly, what they want to become[16]. The latter believes "that Africa must have its own capacity for anticipation

---

10 Cameroonian Laboratory for the Study and Research on Contemporary Societies (CERESC), University of Yaounde 1

11 University of Pennsylvania, Think Tanks and Civil Societies Program, Global Go to Think Tank Index Report, 2018.

12 Ibidem

13 Felwine Sarr, Afrotopia, Paris, Philippe Rey, 2016

14 Achile Mbembe, « Sortir de la grande nuit », Paris, Editions La Découverte, 2013.

15 Founded in September 2015 by Gilles Yabi, Beninese economist and political scientist.

16 On the occasion of the Senegalese presidential elections of February 24, 2019, WATHI, in partnership with the Konrad Adenauer Foundation, created a website dedicated to informing citizens about the stakes of the elections in order to enable them to make an informed choice.

and foresight".[17] Sarr evokes the "alternative modernities" that cannot be fixed in a mimetic relationship between Africans and Europe.[18]

Other groups that have contributed to our reflection and analysis include the African Economic Research Consortium of Kenya, the African Center for Economic Transformation; the Center for Policy and Education of Ghana; the Ethiopian Development Research Institute; the Center for Development and Enterprise of South Africa; the Dakar Engaged Citizen Movement; the Mo Ibrahim Foundation, which focuses on leadership and governance issues; the Tony Elumelu Foundation, named after the famous Nigerian banker who has made $100 million available to African start-ups; the Marakech21 Foundation, dedicated to sustainable development in rural areas; Ghana's influential Center for Policy and Education and its important social studies; the Real Madrid Foundation in Ethiopia, dedicated to education through sport; and the Kenya Institute for Public Policy, which has produced important analyses of the effects of climate change on agricultural production.

Many of the perspectives identified by these African think tanks are supported by regional or continental bodies, including the African Union[19] and the International Chamber of Commerce in Africa (CICA) along with its eight commissions.

Ultimately, the continent's current march towards prosperity and digitization will bust the stereotypes that limit Africa and the way the continent is seen, analyzed and rated. We will demonstrate this later. This march contributes and will contribute to the development of the continent's own capital, including its human capital, in addition to the transformation of its economies and their convergence. It accelerates and will continue to accelerate the ongoing shift from necessity entrepreneurship to opportunity entrepreneurship. Ultimately, it will transform African governance that "is poor because Africa is poor"[20], in the words of Jeffrey Sachs. In this way, it will rebalance the attention between the economic, the social and the political, attention so long diverted by the extreme lack, source of all headlong flights and abundant regressions. Finally, this march forward feeds and will feed the

17 Sabine Cessou, « Afrique: l'émergence n'est ni un plan, ni un produit », RFI, 15 May 2015.

18 Felwine Sarr, Idem.

19 African Union Commission, Boosting Intra-African Trade, January 2012.

20 Sachs, Jeffrey, "The End of Poverty, Economic Possibilities for Our Time", The Penguin Press, NY, 2005

metamorphosis of the continent's historical, social and cultural narrative, as well as that of its communication and representation, which fortunately and normally are gradually being taken over by Africans themselves.

The shift in wealth and the universal deployment of the digital age are gradually producing a new global geopolitical ecosystem that is changing the relative situation of every member of that ecosystem, including that of Africa. These mutations have already modified the relationship of the continent with the world and vice versa.

Our second source is made up of studies and prospective analyses of numerous international interest groups, private or parapublic, which have, in sectors that matter, the planet as a space of intervention, or as playing fields. What do these studies and analyses say about the future of Africans, their societies and their continent?

For each of these groups' sectors of activity, we have sought quantitative and qualitative projections. They constitute a formidable breeding ground for drawing up an updated profile of the continent, of its stakes and challenges as interpreted by various operators who also have Africa as a space for their interventions and a lever for their aspirations.

The photography of the continent is the subject of daily information that we are aware of. It provides the ephemeral and often approximate material, to say the least, that feeds the editorial pages and screens of the world. Too often, it prolongs a mental architecture and public discourse referring to an outdated situation. This architecture is still based on the intellectual and cultural structures ingrained in people's minds at the time of colonization, on the categories of official development assistance and the catalogues of conditionalities that constitute its foreword and its afterword.

The radiography of the continent shows a vibrant and lush whole. We see through it many successful or lost initiatives; networks that are forming, passing or that are alive and well; ambitions that are asserting themselves, others that are contracting; movements that are coming together and flows of convergence.

This convergence is the material for this essay. We believe it to be real, dynamic, and bearer of growth and development. Admittedly, not all of them are accomplished. Like shooting stars, some are fleeting, some will remain so. But the constellation of effective and lasting convergences dominates. It feeds an ecosystem that gradually but irrevocably replaces the postcolonial structures of African societies and their representations. These structures have occupied the material and invisible, tangible and cultural, economic and political spaces of Africans and all those who have taken part in the history of their continent over the last two centuries.

In our work, certain elements of these convergences have not been sufficiently retained, such as the requirements of the ecological transition. As we now know, Africa remains one of the continents most vulnerable to climate variability.[21] Since the major Rio Conference, more than a quarter century ago, and the many global conferences up to the COP22, held in Marrakech at the end of 2016, the ecological situation of the continent and the dangers threatening it have been well documented by the Intergovernmental Panel on Climate Change (IPCC). We know the threat of desertification that could afflict the entire greater sub-Saharan region; the effects of verifiable and already ruinous erosion on the eastern, western and southern coasts of the continent; and the impact of high levels of warming on the territories and populations of Central Africa, already adversely affected by the drying up of Lake Chad.

This need to invent a model of sustainable development so often evoked is not supported by Western donors and the multilateral institutions they control. In this field too, Africans will probably find support from Asian partners, particularly Chinese, who are themselves involved in a very large-scale national ecological project.

The central question of this book, which we have asked ourselves throughout, is addressed to these foundations, research groups and international organizations mentioned above. It is also addressed to each of our readers.

What are they telling us about the future of the continent by 2050?

What have they discovered that could contribute to drawing up a prospective profile of the societies that make up the continent and the 2.4 billion people who will inhabit it by the middle of the century?

For our part, we will first examine the overall situation: globalization effects, demographic change and accelerated urbanization, which have marked, mark and will keep on marking the evolution of the continent between now and 2050. Secondly, we will look at the components of wealth production on the continent: new financial partners, evolution of the economic system including investment, financial, economic and commercial services. We will also pay attention to the ongoing changes in specific sectors: renewable energies, air, land and sea transportation modes, among others, and even a space agency.

---

21 IPCC, IPCC Fifth Assessment Report and What it means for Africa? March 2015.

This work is based on the conviction that, in the coming decades, the continent's development will make it the most important building site of the century and one of the engines of global growth, just as Asia was at the junction of the second and third millennia. It is true that much of this development will be a catch-up game. However, it could be accelerated by technological advances in the fields of communication, energy, education and health.

Much of this development will result from the techno-economic and socio-cultural changes taking place in Africa today. It will also come from the advances made by the aforementioned middle class, from the contributions of Africa's youth, of cities and their leaders, and also from agricultural producers who will see the demand for their production grow steadily. A great share of the modernization of the continent's agriculture depends on that demand. It will come from banking, financial and economic institutions, from commercial operators, African advisory groups and professional associations on the continent.

Our objective is to contribute to a better knowledge of the continent and, in particular, to take into account its diversity and its security. It is important to draw out simplistic and dangerous visions that too often ignore or deny these two elements. Thinking about the future of the continent means taking ownership of its constituent diversity and taking into account the work under way to extend the security enjoyed by the vast majority of Africans to all Africans. Hence the following analysis of the continent's diversity and security.

Of African diversity

In the introduction to this book, which will often treat the continent as a whole, which it is, just like Asia, Europe and the Americas are in all their diversity, it is important to remind the reader that Africa is also an impressive symbol of diversity. Here, as elsewhere in the world, we must go far into the past in order to think about the future. Here, as elsewhere, there are things that disappear over time and things that last over time, such as African languages, to give but one example.

The continent has a plurality of civilizations, of spiritual and cultural systems, of metaphysical, cosmological and ethical conceptions; a plurality of systems of governance; a plurality of social systems, including relationships between genders and age groups, different concepts of family and filiation; a plurality of cultural expressions including a profusion of languages, a varied architectural offer, multiple traditions of artistic production. To put it plainly, African peoples are connected to several ancient civilizations that still provide them with some of their conceptions of life, as is the case for Europeans, Asians and indigenous peoples of the world. A Fulani and a Bantu are both African. However, their historical understanding and explanation of the universe, of its origin and of the origins and purpose of life differ profoundly, as does their conception of social organization. Such is the richness of the world.

Diversity stemming as well from the fifty-four countries of the continent, in terms of their size and ethnic composition; their traditional and current political regimes and judicial systems; types of production and consumption; levels of growth and wealth; considerable differences in gross domestic product per capita, from twenty thousand dollars to three hundred dollars; the organization of health care and education; from the levels of employment and unemployment; from age groups where the "youth" category dominates throughout the continent, unlike almost anywhere else in the world, with the exception of South Asia.

The median age is currently nineteen in Africa, twenty-six in India, thirty-five in the United States, thirty-seven in China, forty-two in the European Union, and forty-three in Japan.

Speaking of diversity, the case of African agriculture is interesting, even edifying. This sector is referred to as the one that dominates the labour market, accounting for 55% of it. However, this average covers huge disparities. Indeed, agricultural employment accounts for 80% of the workforce in Burkina Faso, 28% in Nigeria and 6% in South Africa. Beware of continental averages and global statistics!

The physical diversity of the continent requires a brief reminder: forests, which account for 17% of the world's reserves and are its essential lungs; rivers (35), the Bandama, the Bouregreg, the Jubba, the Limpopo, the Nyong, the Ruvuma, the Tana, the Nile and many others that stretch over more than fifty thousand kilometres and flow into the four seas that surround Africa; summits that reach for the heavens, Kilimanjaro, Gessi, Dashan, Fako Peak, Meru, Muhabura, Tahat, Nimba, Agou among many others; many vibrant deserts that affect 50% of the countries of the continent, including the great sea of sand that stretches over seventy-two thousand square kilometres.

This diversity of Africa is a primary and constitutive feature of the continent.

On the security of the continent

The question of security is part of the overall requirements of the world and, therefore, of Africa. A lack of it is unfortunately spread all over the world, from the bloody Middle East to the Ukraine, from the China Sea to the convulsions affecting certain Central American countries. It is also present in some of the continent's fifty-four countries, including the Democratic Republic of Congo,[22] the Central African Republic, Burundi, Sudan and a few others. It also occurs in countries immediately south of the Sahara or in the Lake Chad region which are affected by the destructive actions of radical Islamists, as are other regions of the world, notably the Middle East and Europe.

This question of security was not taken into account in the preparation of this book as it calls for skills and networks that we do not master. However, we have taken an interest in the current development of security policy on the continent, as desired by the member governments of the Union that brings them and the international community together.

This new security policy is based on the conviction that Africans must gradually assume responsibility for the maintenance of peace and security on their continent. This idea of an African march towards security sovereignty is necessary for various reasons, depending on whether one is African or a foreigner. It would appear that the international community is suffering from a certain fatigue in relation to the maintenance of peace in Africa and that some Africans, for their part, are anxious to gradually exercise full control over such a sensitive and decisive sector. Hence the initiatives taken by the African Union to implement these complementary expectations.

These include the creation of the African Standby Force (ASF) housed in Douala and its draft version, the African Capacity for Immediate Response to Crises (ACIRC). This initiative aims to provide the continent, in the long term, with an intervention tool that can prevent or resolve various internal or external conflicts, such as the one affecting the Democratic Republic of Congo. For this implementation, Africans can count on the support of its historical European and wider Western partners, as well as that of China. Indeed, Beijing is showing a growing interest in the security of a continent where its interests have become major. The Russian Federation is also seeking its niche in this policy, which is inseparable from the vast arms market represented by the countries of the continent.

---

22 According to The Economist, this conflict "has cost more lives than any other conflict since the 1940s, more lives than the wars in Syria, Iraq, Vietnam or Korea. « Congo is sliding back to bloodshed », *The Economist*, February 17th, 2018.

In time, this force could probably prevail in the face of threats of a different nature, such as those embodied by Boko Haram or Al Qaeda over vast regions of the Sahara or at the junction of Central and West Africa.

Before President Sarkozy set fire to the Libyan volcano and transformed its national territory into a "hub of all traffics", this country, which holds the continent's largest oil reserves and owns one of the fifteen largest sovereign wealth funds in the world,[23] the security situation on the continent appeared less deteriorated compared to Asia (Near and Middle East). This situation has certainly changed since the assassination of Muammar Gaddafi in 2011. However, we must not lose sight of the fact that, in this vast continent, terrorist attacks remain confined to known territories, and that the vast majority of countries on the continent and of Africans are in no way affected by this terrifying use of terror.

23 R. Yonga, Guide des Fonds Souverains Africains – African Markets

Chapter One

GLOBAL TRANSFORMATION AND AFRICA

The wealth shift towards the East and the South

The migration of wealth from the West to the East and the South of the planet is entrenching the continent in the South-South financial, economic and commercial networks.[24] These networks, the most performing on our planet, are the engine of world growth today and for the foreseeable future. This positioning opens up far-reaching convergences. As the President of China said at the BRICS[25] Forum in Johannesburg in July 2018: "New growth drivers have replaced the old ones."

This contributes to the emancipation of Africans and their historical relations with the western part of the world and its components: governments, media, churches, armies, national, regional or international public institutions, governments, non-governmental organizations etc. The African intellectual class evokes this emancipation in many ways. For Cameroonian historian Achile Mbembe, it is a matter of "cultural decolonization". It is a matter of "purging Africans of the desire for Europe". This cannot be, either philosophically or culturally, the whole of the African condition." No one pleads for an impossible banishment of the relationship with the European continent, even if many, such as Achile Mbenbe, do not hesitate to affirm that "seen from Europe, Africa is only a great Bantustan. "It is undeniable that, from

24 OCDE, Idem.

25 Brazil, Russia, India, China and South Africa.

now on, this relationship is part of a global whole that includes it and goes beyond it on a long-term basis.[26]

This historical relationship has not yielded sufficient growth and development over the past two or three hundred years. To this day, of the twenty-eight poorest countries in the world, twenty-seven are in sub-Saharan Africa. To quote the President of Ghana: "It has not worked and it will not work."[27]

Echoing these statements, the Financial Times observed in late August 2018 that the spectacular growth of the China-Africa relationship has enabled Beijing to encourage other emerging nations in turn to look at Africa with different eyes. On the heels of the Chinese, Brazilians, Indians, Russians and Turks, among others, have all intensified their courtship" of the continent. This has had the net effect of shaking up "an old and fraying order dominated by cautious western donors and former colonial powers, prompting the most significant shift in the continent's relations with the outside world since the end of the cold war."[28]

These movements combined have pulled African economies upwards. Between 2016 and 2020, nearly 50% of the continent's countries are expected to experience growth between 5% and 8%.

Such are the consequences of the wealth shift from the West towards the planet's East and South. These consequences have shattered the occidental mould of the world. They have globalized the capacity to produce science and its most advanced technological applications, from artificial intelligence to giga-data, from quantum computing to biotechnology. In short, they have globalized the capacity to produce growth and wealth. The world's economy, including world trade, has been disrupted and, at its core, displaced.

This far-reaching geopolitical reversal is finally reaching the continent. It too must eventually benefit from the irreversible linkage between human and artificial intelligence for analysis, forecasting and intervention. It has and will continue to have an incompressible need for that.

Africa and Asia: linked destinies

The total value of trade between Africa, China and India in 2016 was US$177 billion. In that same year, trade dealings between Africa and

26 Jagdish N. Sheth, "Chindia Rising", Incore Publishing LLC, 2011.

27 Nana Akyfo-Addo, Welcome Speech to the President of France, November 30, 2017.

28 "The 21st century Great Game is Africa's to lose", *Financial Times*, August 31, 2018.

Asia as a whole amounted to more than US$200 billion, while trade between Africa, the United States, France and Great Britain reached US$142 billion. China tops this list of countries with the value of its business with Africa accounting for $130 billion, while the continent's trade with the United States and France amounted to $52 billion and $48 billion respectively. This is one of the major consequences of the aforementioned wealth shift. In 2018, fifteen African countries recorded a trade surplus with China.

Another noticeable fact is the favourable evolution of intra-African trade. According to Vera Songwe, Secretary General of the Economic Commission for Africa, intra-African trade has "more than doubled since 2000 and now represents 18% of the continent's commercial transactions", totalling one hundred and fifty billion dollars, an increase of 100% since the beginning of the century. Economists from the University of Saint-Louis in Senegal have done the full calculation of such trade, including transactions in the informal economy. Consequently, the data on inter-state trade on the continent are shifting in level and freeing us from the heavy literature of bilateral cooperation and international institutions on the subject.

Gradually, the countries of the continent are integrating into the global economy through the financial, entrepreneurial and commercial circuits of emerging economies with more flexible and aggressive components than those of their Western competitors. The ever-growing association of African countries with the Asian Infrastructure Investment Bank (AIIB), led by Beijing, reflects this. The same applies to their progressive participation in the new Silk Road, China's mega infrastructure program that links investment and development aid, economic and trade cooperation as well as social and cultural cooperation.

In order to support new sectors driven by population growth, urban development and the needs of the African middle class, such as real estate, construction, insurance, transport, etc., the continent needs an ever-increasing flow of investment. This contribution has mainly come from Asians, especially Chinese, as the current development of intra-continental trade is facilitated by the development of transport infrastructure, financed and developed largely by Chinese companies.

Togolese President Faure Gnassingbe expressed the feeling of many when he stated at the Forum on China-Africa Cooperation (FOCAC) in Beijing in September 2018: "whether we like it or not, China and Africa will share linked fates in the 21st century".

Born with the millennium, this Forum marks a turning point in relations between Beijing and the countries of the African continent.

From an agenda reflecting general affairs and foreseeable cooperation between the partners, it has evolved into a strategic forum to which, in addition to the Secretary-General of the United Nations, representatives of twenty-seven international and regional organizations have been invited.

The agenda of these forums has a new outlook and the identified benchmarks were major: equality between stakeholders, deepening of mutual knowledge and broadening of consultations. Indeed, in addition to the sixty billion dollars of investment announced for the next three years, the Chinese President proposed a vast array of measures: fifty agricultural assistance projects and the provision of five hundred experts in the field; an infrastructure connectivity programme developed with the African Union; trade facilities including the presence of Africans at the China International Import Expo; and fifty thousand additional scholarships for African students; the creation in Africa of a Research and Intervention Centre on climate change, oceans, protection of forests, fauna and flora; fifty major projects in the field of environment; the creation of a Sino-African media cooperation network; the modernization of trade, tax and investment laws and the organization of a Sino-African Forum for Peace and Security.

This impressive platform highlights "interconnected visions" amongst these factions. Special attention should be paid to the seventh proposal related to people-to-people exchanges. It announces the establishment of an Institute of African Studies to strengthen exchanges "on civilization" between China and Africa.[29] Finally, China invites Africans to participate in the International League of Silk Road Theatres, the International Alliance of Silk Road Museums and the Silk Road Arts Festival Network. Enter culture!

The list of convergences is expanding. It now includes the field of security, as recently pointed out by Arthur Banga, the Ivorian specialist in military strategies. In fact, this area was the subject of a first China-Africa Defense and Security Forum, in June 2018, in the Chinese capital.[30]

As noted earlier, Africans are integrating themselves into the financial and commercial circuits of these economies, which have been experiencing continuous growth over the last forty years, from 21% of the global aggregate in 1980 to 45% today and could account for

---

29 Martina Bassan, « Expertise et recherche chinoise sur l'Afrique », in *Afrique contemporaine*, 2014/2.

30 Arthur Banga, « Surfons sur la vague chinoise », *Jeune Afrique*, no 3020, November 25th – December 1st 2018.

more than 50% of that global aggregate by 2030. This provides a great deal of opportunity, including closer cooperation with the EMPEA, the global industry association for private capital in emerging markets, for instance. Such membership opens the doors to many important investment funds, and enables discussions with global corporations in emerging countries. These multinationals represented 5% of the famous Global 500 of the world's leading multinationals in 1990, and are expected to reach 45% in 2025. In time, they will give rise to multiple global production chains (value chains) which increasingly should include African partners. These convergences or integrations can be seen today in Morocco, Ethiopia, Egypt, Kenya, Nigeria, Rwanda, Côte d'Ivoire, etc.

On a completely different level, this rapprochement between Asian and African economic partners will offer the latter a grip on the optimism of emerging countries, especially China, which, according to journalist Laurent Alexandre, "contrasts with the deep pessimism of Europeans, especially the French".[31] Meanwhile, Hélène Carrère d'Encausse evokes a "triumphant Asia" towards which "the geopolitical weight is shifting." The member of the Académie française argues in favour of maintaining the link between Europe and Russia because "to ignore it, to turn one's back on it means for Europe to cut itself off from Asia, that is to say staying away from the great geopolitical upheaval of the 21st century.»[32]

Africa as a Market

The vitality of the continental market has expanded, as barometers of growing economic activity indicate. These barometers include land, sea and air transport; they will be expounded upon further in this work. Other sectors such as renewable energy, agriculture and agri-food, urban development, industrial and residential construction, traditional retail and e-commerce, insurance, health services including pharmaceuticals, and financial services continue to grow exponentially.

These developments in the African market are undeniable and unprecedented. Their convergence is producing a powerful dynamic, an unrivalled volume of business, levels of employment and wealth that the continent urgently needs. These developments will be acceler-

---

31 Laurent Alexandre, « La fin du monde? Pas tout de suite! » *L'Express*, February 14th 2018.

32 Hélène Carrère d'Encausse, "Il ne faut pas juger le pouvoir autoritaire de Poutine à l'aune de nos seuls critères", *Le Figaro*, Sunday, March 18 2018.

ated by the consolidation of regional markets. It is, after all, unreasonable to want to fully develop the economy in countries with very small demographics. In twenty-five countries of the continent, the population is less than ten million; in nineteen, it is less than five million.

If the current pace is maintained in the coming decades, it will place Africa in the global average for the progression in living standards and above this average in terms of their contributions to global economic growth. To be sure, too many Africans will still suffer from poverty, but an ever-increasing majority of Africans will be lifted out of it. The horizon of a continent freed from "want" is now conceivable.

The gradual growth of a market of solvent consumers on the continent could, by mid-century, occupy, along with those of China and India, the very top ranks of the world's consumer markets. Between 2000 and 2020, consumption on the continent has grown significantly: four hundred and seventy billion dollars in 2000, 1.1 trillion dollars in 2020. In this context, it is not surprising to see the multiplication of shopping centres on the continent. In 2016, Sagaci Research, a firm specializing in Africa, counted 587 of them in Sub-Saharan Africa, of which 383 are in operation and 204 are scheduled to open in 2020.[33]

This supply of goods and services will only grow. Demographic and urban development, coupled with the expansion of economic activities, will drive up consumption in all key areas: food, education, housing, consumer goods, leisure, health, financial services and telecommunications for the former; agribusiness, insurance, industry, construction, transport, wholesale trade, natural resources, banking, telecommunications and communications technology in the latter. This growing consumption will serve as a lever for African production. In the food sector, which includes agribusiness, the aim must be to achieve the self-sufficiency sought by every and all countries.

At the Africa CEO Forum in March 2018, the volume of consumption on the continent expected by 2030 was estimated at 6.7 trillion dollars, of which 2.5 trillion (almost a third) was for household consumption and 4.2 for business expenditure.[34]

How many "solvent" or middle-class consumers will that be in 2050's Africa?

They would be between three hundred and fifty and four hundred million today, i.e. almost a third of the continent's current population. They could reach 1.1 billion in 2050, or nearly 45% of the population, to be interested by the major Asian, European, American and Afri-

33 https://africanmanager.com

34 Ecofin Hebdo, March 30 2018.

can brands, in addition to visiting the world just as the 150 million Chinese tourists, children and grandchildren of some of the poorest generations in China's history, do today.

For the first time, in 2017, the Consumer Class Conditions Index (CCCI) included the continent's countries in its work to measure and classify global purchasing power. The result is ambiguous. It shows that in Africa, the distribution of the wealth created remains uncertain but that purchasing power is growing inexorably.[35]

This vast and diverse future market constitutes a major bargaining chip for Africans in negotiations with partners around the world. Access to this market should be limited to other countries that will fully consider the interests of Africans as part of trade agreements. The Togolese economist Kako Nubukpo holds a similar viewpoint when he evokes "the increased circulation of goods made in Africa".

As will be explored further, the benefits derived from the relations of Africans with new sustainable partners, the gradual consolidation of their regional markets and the new prospects opening up on the continental market are manifold. In particular, they provide access to patient capital that the continent has always lacked and that the Chinese government, institutions and enterprises have offered over the past two decades. China's rise in Africa is partly explained by the availability of large amounts of credit in terms of volume, cost and duration over time.

This series of movements is steadily improving the living standards of several hundred million Africans. Admittedly, this will not occur simultaneously or at the same pace in all regions of the continent. As in Eastern Europe, after the glasnost policy initiated by Mikhail Gorbachev and the implosion of the Soviet Union, and as in China after the policy of openness and the four modernizations implemented by Deng Xiaoping, poverty is and will keep being reduced gradually in Africa. It will be curtailed first and foremost in cities, some of which are called "global", and also in certain regions and countries favoured by their geographical position and their access to regional, continental and world markets. It will be progressively curtailed in rural areas in response to the growing demand for agricultural products, a direct consequence of demographic and urbanization trends.

These areas should normally benefit from advantages negotiated with investors, wherever they may be from. These advantages should include technology transfer and, at all levels, the integration of the

35 "Markets – Looking Beyond GDP", Harvard Business Review, January-February, 2018.

African labour force in all major works. Then poverty will be alleviated and, with it, the procession of "fear and want."

The question of governance is decisive. The essential convergences previously identified need to be supported, updated, completed and implemented with rigour and consistency. The continent needs strategic governments capable of meticulous steering based entirely on national, regional and continental interests. Then Africa will fully play its scientific and technological, economic and financial, social and cultural part. The Asian revolution that marked the end of the previous century and changed the course of the world will be followed by the African revolution. It will take place in the first half of this century and will emerge at the junction of multiple convergences that can be seen in the current stage of African history.

The gradual integration of Africa

Although photographs of the continent may reveal many detestable asperities, as in all other parts of the world, its more revealing X-rays display for their part an effervescence that contrasts with Africa's prevailing negative representations in the West, particularly in Europe. This vibrancy can be seen in many areas.

Among others, one thinks of the reforms relating to the needs of investors and entrepreneurs. In 2017, according to the World Bank, a third of the reforms carried out across the world in these fields have taken place in sub-Saharan Africa.[36]

One also considers the establishment of economic and commercial areas better adapted to the demands of the times, as a way to erase the calamitous effects of borders resulting from colonization.

The former Secretary-General of the Boao Forum for Asia, Zhou Wenzhong, explains the economic development of Asia as a result of the changing relationships between the region's economies, more specifically the gradual advance of their interdependence. In doing so, they have put an end to a long period when the volume of their trade with America exceeded the volume of their trade with each other and have entered a period when trade between themselves exceeds that with the United States.[37]

Truth in Asia, truth in Africa!

---

36 The World Bank, "Doing Business 2019: A Year of Record Reforms, Rising Influence", October 31, 2018.

37 Zhou Wenzhong, "Creating New Miracles in Asia, China Focus", a special feature produced by Beijing Review.

Initially, the countries of the continent created regional communities such as the Southern African Development Community (SADC), which has the highest rate of trade integration on the continent, followed by the Economic Community of West African States (ECOWAS), the Common Market for Eastern and Southern Africa (COMESA) and the Economic and Monetary Community of Central Africa (CEMAC). More than acknowledged but less than desired, these country groupings have taken steps in the right direction, particularly in Southern, West and East Africa. In recent years, far-reaching initiatives have been taken to recognize the indispensable complementarities between Africa's national and regional economies.

The Sharm el-Sheikh Agreement

In June 2015, twenty-six East African countries signed a free trade treaty. This so-called "Tripartite" treaty stretches from Cape Town, South Africa, to Cairo, Egypt and includes three regions or communities: COMESA, SADC and the East African Community (EAC). These twenty-six countries make up a total of six hundred and fifty million people. Together, they have an overall gross domestic product (GDP) of nearly one trillion euros. It has been estimated that the expected increase in trade resulting from their new agreement is 25%.

The Kigali Agreement

The Kigali Agreement of March 2018, which creates a continental free trade area (CFTA), is a decisive step in the establishment of economic and trade areas that are better adapted to the demands of the times.[38] As a result, the continent appears for what it is, a breeding ground of multiple resources certainly, but also one of the most important economic and commercial areas in the world.[39] Consequently, it should find its place in international production and value chains. According to estimates by the World Economic Forum, the implementation of the Agreement could, in less than ten years, increase intra-African trade by 52%.[40]

---

38 The agreement has been signed by 44 countries on the continent and must be ratified by national parliaments. It comes into force when ratified by at least 22 countries.

39 In his 1960 book *Black Africa: The Economic and Cultural Basis for a Federated State* (Présence africaine), Cheikh Anta Diop had already shed light on the fertility of a continental market.

40 Landry Signé, Africa has a new trade area. This is what you need to know. World Economic Forum – Africa. The Convention, April 3, 2018.

At maturity, the CFTA opens access to a market of 1.2 billion people, 1.7 billion in 2030 and 2.4 billion in 2050, for an African trade flow of one trillion dollars in 2017.[41] These data justify the accelerated implementation of the largest agreement, with regards to the number of participants, since the creation of the World Trade Organization. Nevertheless, as we see in the case of Europe, economic integration is not enough.[42] It needs a socio-cultural ecosystem to avoid being depleted of its substance which is, as Kako Nubukpo reminds us, the answer to this simple question: "What do Africans want to do together?".

The Agreement should trigger a virtuous circle. Indeed, more intra-African trade should produce structural transformations of economies, promote the development of production, the enrichment of production, the extension of research and job creation. Even if accelerated, these transformations will be gradual, since they depend on a number of factors: the increase and diversification of production; improvement of transport infrastructure; streamlining of procedures and abolition of existing customs duties. Important work is being carried out in all these areas. The heavyweights of the economy, South Africa, Morocco, Egypt and Kenya have all agreed, with the exception of Nigeria, which has not yet joined the forty-four signatory countries.[43]

In addition to plans of emergence that have been developed by a majority of countries on the continent, we also note important statements of regional or continental ambitions. Thus, from Morocco to Djibouti, from Rwanda to Botswana, from Côte d'Ivoire to Kenya, from Ethiopia to Ghana and from Senegal to Tunisia, the profile of another Africa is being drawn. One that strives to be enterprising, ambitious and conquering, capable of appropriating and using advanced technologies and of competing with African or international competitors. These projections will remain wishful thinking if indigenous and international investments do not follow, hence the importance we attribute to those in this work.

Regional and continental integration is gradually taking place. Its implementation depends on the intervention and repeated demands of multiple actors. Indeed, an ever-increasing number of African financial, economic, commercial and professional groups operate on a regional or even multi-regional basis in Africa. They

---

41 Afreximbank – African Export-Import Bank, *African Trade Report, 2017*.

42 Pierre Moscovici, « Il est minuit en Europe », Paris, Grasset, 2016.

43 As of January 1st 2019.

have a direct, high and lasting interest in achieving integration objectives. Their requests and pressures should, among other things, drive matters forward.

Furthermore, the implementation of many major projects undeniably contributes to a form of "functional regional integration", in the words of Abdoul Salam Bello[44]; from the electricity interconnection between five West African countries, whose access to that energy resource will benefit 294 localities[45], to the 750-kilometre railway line linking Addis Ababa to the port of Djibouti; to the 470-kilometre railway line linking Nairobi to the port of Mombasa, which could potentially serve four neighbouring countries in the consolidation of a West African network that could serve six countries in the greater region. Other major projects are in the process of being developed, such as the four-thousand-kilometre-long Trans-Saharan gas pipeline that would link Nigeria and Morocco and which was recently relaunched by King Mohammed VI on the occasion of the visit to Rabat of the Nigerian President, Muhammadu Buhari.

Africa in the Digital Age

The second global change, i.e. the universal deployment of the digital age, gives Africans their place in the innumerable communication, knowledge, production and exchange networks that structure the digital civilization, the real gateway for humanity in the third millennium. It makes them members of digital humanity without the historical intermediaries who, for centuries, have shielded them from global scientific and technological change. This screen is fading slowly but surely. The direction is clear. "Technology in Africa is making great strides", says Jonathan Rosenthal in a special report from *The Economist* in 2017".[46] The following year, Jack Ma, the founder of Alibaba, proposed an end destination for those strides in a sibylline formula: "Let's make Africa a digital Africa". After investigation, *Jeune Afrique* magazine argued that "while the means are still lacking, Africa has never been more present on the world scientific scene, and many talents are emerging". The issue was headlined "Science and technology:

---

[44] Abdoul Salam Bello, « La régionalisation en Afrique: Essai sur un processus d'intégration et de développement », Paris, L'Harmattan, 2017.

[45] Benin, Nigeria, Niger, Burkina Faso and Togo. The network is enriched by the production of solar voltaic energy, wind energy and biomass.

[46] "The leapfrog model, What technology can do for Africa", Special Report, *The Economist*, November 10th 2017.

the end of complexes."[47] At the same time, the Islamic Development Bank launched the "Transformers Roadshow" in 2018, a program to promote science and technology on the continent.

With over one billion Internet users, Africa will become one of the world's three great digital communities by mid-century, along with India and China, perhaps the largest in terms of numbers.

Convergences are at the basis of this first-time achievement in the modern and contemporary period: the full participation of Africans in the scientific and technological evolution of humanity, the access and control of all reception, production and dissemination media that carry all the variety of messages, information, scientific or cultural products available on the Web. Such participation and access have been made possible thanks to dynamic partnerships, in particular with regard to technological products from Asia that have been adapted to the capacities and needs of various clienteles, in particular young Africans.

This transition helps bust the stereotypes that enclave Africa and the way the continent is seen and appreciated. It also produces a shift in the global economic and technological map and, in so doing, "shapes the future of the world".[48] On a global scale, these convergences are inclusive. They are Asian, Latin American, European and North American. They are also African.

Ultimately, they gradually rebalance the focus between the economic and the political, focus which in the past was almost exclusively absorbed by politics. Instead of being an appendix to foreign analyses, they are leading Africans to debate political and ethical issues from their own experiences. As such, CIPESA[49] summits examine the state of Internet freedom on the continent. Finally, they fuel the metamorphosis of the continent's historical, social and cultural narrative, as well as its communication and representation, which is "extraordinarily unchanging despite its profound changes and societal dynamics." [50]

As previously noted, these extensive and far-reaching convergences are gradually producing a new planetary geopolitical ecosystem that involves a variety of players, including Africa. These changes have already reshaped the continent's relationship with the world.

During the long colonial era and until the end of the previous century, the continent's human and natural wealth served as a mag-

---

47 Olivier Marbot, Quentin Velluel et Nadoun Coulibaly, « Sciences et technologies, la fin des complexes », *Jeune Afrique*, no 3018, November 11-17 2018.

48 Guy Taillefer, « Réussir la transition », *Le Devoir*, 14 août 2017.

49 The Collaboration on international ICT Policy for East and Southern Africa.

50 Felwine Sarr, op.cit., 2016.

net, especially for Europeans. This interest is not extinguished today. It still looks hungrily at resources such as uranium from Namibia, bauxite from Guinea, Angolan and Nigerian oil, copper, cobalt and coltan from the Democratic Republic of Congo, nickel from Cameroon, etc. Today, this interest has become part of a larger whole that includes the current and virtual market, now its main force of attraction, as was the case for China at the turn of the millennium. That is the real difference between Africa's relationship with Europe and Africa's relationship with Asia: a resource reservoir in the first case; a resource reservoir in the second, but also a market, i.e. a system of exchanges between these two partners that opens up a whole range of global partnerships.

These major advances undoubtedly explain why, according to a remarkable study by Deloitte, "Africa is now the world's second fastest growing economic region after Asia".[51]

These positions call for a profound transformation of the governance and economy of the continent, a process that has been the subject of important forward-looking work by the African Union Commission. That Commission, which will celebrate its centenary in 2063, has carried out an extensive consultation, studying trends and scenarios of possible futures for a continent that will be "the most populous in the world" by that time, and which has the potential to become "a powerful and influential partner on the world stage."[52]

Agenda 2063 was born out of this exploratory work. The exercise was severely judged by some who would have preferred the attention to be placed on the immediate emergencies of the continent and their priority over prospective analyses. These critics would be more credible if, at the same time, they did not rush to Brussels, Washington or Beijing to try to shed light on their own future. Does Africa also have the right to its own prospective studies with its own margins of error and its own aims? Could it, like the other continental entities of the planet, Europe, Asia, Latin America, etc., project itself into the future without the heavy and often incompetent interference of certain international organizations that have in the past merged dubious analyses and destructive conditionalities?

An accelerated digital transition

At a time when digital activity accounts for 22% of the world economy, nearly 40% in 2050, and today contributes 3.7% of the GDP

---

51 Deloitte, « La consommation en Afrique. Le marché du XXIe siècle », 2015

52 African Union Commission, "Agenda 2063, The Africa We Want", Adis Adeba, 2015.

of advanced economies, according to the fourth Internet conference, Africa is also experiencing a far-reaching digital transition.[53]

According to a Deloitte study, *"La consommation en Afrique"*, the majority of Africans have a mobile subscription and 30% have a smartphone connection. Nearly one in five young Africans has already purchased a product or service with their mobile phone. In 2017, the top ten telephone operators on the continent saw their income increase. This is not surprising seeing as the African market is the most buoyant in the world, according to the World Association of Telecom Operators (WATO).[54]

The quality of the connection is also steadily improving. While in 2015, 75% of African Internet users had to be content with 2G access and 21% with 3G access, by 2025, 7% will be dependent on 2G access, 70% on 3G, 21% on 4G and 3% on 5G. There is much more to these developments than just statistics. They should be seen as evidence of a gradual convergence of systems towards 4G and 5G. There is a latent, far-reaching battle between Nokia and Ericsson, the pioneers in the installation of technological infrastructures, and the Chinese company Huawei, which will seek to consolidate its gains on the continent. At the end of the day, billions of dollars and large-scale partnerships in numerous fields.

A little more every day, Africans are establishing themselves as that third most important virtual digital community in the world, as mentioned above. The benefits are visible. A senior international civil servant who has no particular link with Africa agrees: "You can see the impact of technological developments in many areas. In agriculture, we are seeing an improvement in crop yields through the use of technological devices that inform farmers about the state of the soil. Access to finance is much wider thanks to mobile banking. The use of transport is improving thanks to the development of applications." According to Mark Zuckerberg, this is where the future is being built. Yet the present is already impressive. According to the 2019 report of the International Mobile Telephone Operators Association (GSMA), a report on the digital economy in Africa, mobile technologies contribute up to 7.1% to the continent's gross domestic product. In monetary terms, this percentage corresponds to one hundred and ten billion dollars.[55]

53 Assises de la transformation digitale en Afrique (6th edition), 2017

54 « Telecom: Le temps de la relance », *Jeune Afrique*, Hors-série, no.48, 2018.

55 Jephté Tchemedie, « Selon la GSMA, les technologies mobiles contribuent à 7,1% au PIB ». *Digital business Africa*, January 22th, 2018.

As head of the international section of *The Asian Banker*, David Gyori says that the time has come for digital Africa and that the continent has considerable advantages to succeed in this transition.[56] These assessments are shared by many, including the World Bank, which by 2018 has contributed $25 billion to the digitalization of the continent. The benefits cited by David Gyori are tangible.

- A predominantly young population inclined to accept, master and prefer digital solutions.
- A fast-growing population that constitutes a constant flow of available first-generation clients; progress in schooling, a prerequisite for mastering and using communication technologies. To that is added specialized training by regional, continental and international organizations, non-governmental organizations, specialized institutes and private companies.
- The rise of a middle class whose size varies according to evaluations but whose continuous growth is unanimously accepted. The new urban environment of the continent conducive to trade, especially online trade. Google, for instance, has already brought one million young Africans under its Digital Skills banner.
- The vastness of the continent and the variable quality of its means of transportation and communication ensure that digital solutions have considerable comparative advantages.
- Finally, the continued growth of virtual identity goes hand in hand with a financial identity. The latter is the seed for the financial inclusion of the economy's informal sector. According to the Executive Secretary of the New Partnership for Africa's Development (NEPAD), "this virtual identity is all that the informal sector needs to fully integrate into the formal economy[57]". The consequence is considerable. Indeed, the contribution of the informal economy to the GDP varies, depending on the country, from 30% to 90% in sub-Saharan Africa. David Gyori, implores Africans to embrace the "digital revolution" underway in Asia and reject the "digital evolution" that is the approach of the West. "In many ways, he adds, the continent's economy and Africans will be substantially enriched."

The growing investments and diverse contributions of the major groups in the digital economy in Africa are still not at the level of their

---

[56] David Gyori, "Africa's ten key advantages in digital transition", *The Asian Banker*, February 23, 2018.

[57] Ibrahim Assane Mayaki, « L'identité virtuelle, une étale vers l'inclusion financière », *Jeune Afrique*, no. 2997, June 17-23 2018.

current and foreseeable revenues on the continent. However, after a long period of apparent indifference, they are finally interested in a clientele that could account for a quarter of humanity in the future.

In 2015, better late than never, Facebook opened an office in South Africa and, from there, is rolling out or planning to roll out its development plan to markets of not only the country of Mandela, but also those of Nigeria, Kenya, Senegal, Côte d'Ivoire, Ghana, Tanzania, Rwanda, Uganda, Zambia, Mozambique and Ethiopia. Today, "Free Basics", the controversial Internet service launched by Facebook[58], is present in 23 countries on the continent and serves 84 million African users.

In 2018, following Mark Zuckerberg's trip in Africa, Facebook opened a Technology Centre in Nigeria, a centre dedicated to the development of skills in the fields of artificial intelligence, augmented reality, machine learning and the Internet of Things.

Meanwhile, Google has facilities in seven countries on the continent.[59] The company has major programs there: Google Go for Internet access in twenty-six countries; Launchpad Accelerator Africa to support the financing and development of technology start-ups; Digify Bytes and Digify Pro, which offer training in digital marketing, search engine optimization and corporate governance in the digital age, among other topics. Google is also contributing to the development of fibre optic networks in Ghana and Uganda. Finally, as a counterweight to the Centre created by Facebook in Nigeria, Google has opened an artificial intelligence research centre in Ghana, the Google AI Research Center. The mission of this centre is to support African researchers working to combine artificial intelligence with the sciences of health, education and agriculture.

Microsoft Africa has installations in forty countries on the continent. The company is conducting numerous programs there as a result of the 4Afrika initiative, which aims to facilitate affordable access to the Internet. In addition, between 2013 and 2017, Microsoft has supported thousands of small and medium enterprises, more than a third of which are online; it trained 800,000 technicians in new technologies and provided financial support to more than 100 start-ups in the field. Finally, Microsoft Africa has set up data centres in Johannesburg and Cape Town, which have the capacity to cover a good half of the continent.

---

58 « En Afrique, l'internet gratuit grâce à Facebook, mais à quel prix? » TV5, August 3 2017. https://information.tv5monde.com

59 These countries are: Senegal, Ghana, Nigeria, South Africa, Kenya, Uganda and Egypt.

As for Amazon Inc., it has made an attempt to integrate the continent by taking control, in 2017, of the Moroccan company Souq.com, the leader in online commerce in North Africa and the Middle East. By the summer of 2018, speculation was raging about Amazon.com's move into South Africa.

In almost every country on the continent, institutes, schools, and incubators are hosting large numbers of young people wishing to take their projects and activities in the digital economy. The MELT in Accra, a subsidiary of Meltwater, a Swedish multinational specializing in online data analysis, is emblematic of these institutions. It is a school of computer science, an entrepreneurial academy and an incubator for young companies all at once.

Finally, to conclude this inventory of the presence in Africa of the major Western companies in the field, it is worth noting the initiatives taken by Netflix: opening of a studio in Nigeria, the launch of Netflix in South Africa in 2015, and its extension to the entire continent the following year. Similarly to India[60], the company had two million subscribers in 2018 and is targeting ten million in 2030.

Chinese companies in the field are not to be outdone. China has chosen Zimbabwe to test its facial recognition projects for dark-skinned faces, while Alibaba has just set up a regional online sales platform in Kigali.

One billion African Internet users

Within a quarter of a century, the universal deployment of the digital age has extended its magisterium to almost all human societies, their institutions and organizations, as well as to enterprises producing goods and services in the public and private sectors. The digital age has also conquered a majority of humans, 54% of whom have become Internet users, i.e. four billion one hundred and twelve million people, by the end of 2018. They could be six billion by 2050. With the highest growth rate in the world, 20% between January 2017 and January 2018, the number of African Internet users reached four hundred and thirty-five million at the beginning of 2019. The continent is gradually catching up.

Africans have gradually appropriated the range of services carried by digital technology and have taken steps to access them. The road ahead is certainly considerable, just like the one that's already been travelled.

60 "Netflix has brought Hollywood to its knees. Beating Bollywood may be harder", *Blomberg Businessweek*, July 2, 2018.

With more than 800 million subscribers, i.e. 70% growth since 2010, mobile telephony on the continent is at a comparable level with almost all regions of the world.[61] For the first time in their history, hundreds of millions of Africans have access to a modern means of communication. This extraordinary breakthrough was made possible by the ability of Asia, particularly China, India, and to a lesser extent Indonesia and Vietnam, to offer exceptional quantities of technological products, including adapted smart phones at affordable prices for masses of African consumers.[62] This availability has created a huge ecosystem conducive to the invention and deployment of technology services tailored to the needs of Africans by African start-ups for communication, education, healthcare, etc. In 2017, 52% of mobile payments worldwide will be made on the continent. In this field, Africa is the world leader.

As for network penetration, it has been growing exponentially since the beginning of the century. Banks, insurance companies, distributors and sellers of goods and services are increasingly relying, here as elsewhere in the world, on the insights provided by algorithms based on metadata collections.

Africa now has 435 million Internet users. By the middle of the century, they could total more than a billion. They will then outnumber European and North American Internet users combined. Along with India and China, they will occupy, in terms of numbers, the very first ranks. Both actual and virtual, this critical mass encourages investment, innovation and transactional activity in its many forms.

In its 2017 special report mentioned above, *The Economist* reminds us that technology in Africa is making huge advances and that in the sub-Saharan part of the continent, countries are on the verge of a change driven by it. As a result, Africans will be healthier, wealthier and better educated. The following year, the 2018 Africa CEO Forum rightly evoked the possibility of making digital developments an unprecedented economic springboard for African private sector companies.

As mentioned earlier, the doubling of the continent's population is forecasted by 2050. It will then total two billion four hundred million inhabitants, or one out of four human beings in the world. One billion of them will be less than eighteen years old. If Africa keeps going and counts seven hundred and fifty million urban dwellers in 2030, there

---

[61] 215 million mobile phones were sold on the continent in 2016.

[62] Jeff Muskus – David Rocks, "Setting the pace in Africa's phone market". *Businessweek*, April 2018.

will be one billion two hundred million in 2050.[63] As for the middle class, estimated today at three hundred and fifty million people, equivalent to that of China, it would total five hundred million people in 2030 and one billion in 2050.

These overall forecasts are of paramount importance for Africans and for humanity at large. They outline part of their future, which is inseparable from ours; this is an essential convergence.

Demographic affluence

No forward-looking analysis of Africa can avoid the demographic issue, since it so obviously informs overall projections about the future of the continent and its inhabitants. Along with South Asia, the African continent is the area in which significant demographic enrichment will take place throughout the century.

Almost all of the two billion human beings who will be born by 2050 will be born in these two major regions of the world. In Africa, the curve is unambiguous, from two hundred and eighty-five million in 1960 to one billion two hundred and fifty million in 2017, and two billion four hundred million in 2050.

For some, the demographic enrichment announced belongs to the category of cataclysms that must be contained because, in their opinion, its effects would be catastrophic for the continent and the international community. According to the demographer Hervé le Bras, "some people are anxious about a galloping population, which is a convenient way for the countries of the North not to question their consumption. By blaming the countries of the South for having more children, the rich countries are in reality telling them that they don't have the right to pollute or consume as much."[64]

The demographic enrichment of the continent is a precious asset for others, the author of this work among them. It is true that the West allows the age balance of its populations to deteriorate and avoids the subject, which has become taboo. China, by contrast, is making the demographic question a matter of state. It has just reversed its one-child policy and authorized an increase in births, given the current ageing of its population.[65]

---

63 Sommet Africités: 1,2 milliard d'urbains en 2050, le nouveau défi africain. www.africites.org

64 Hervé le Bras, *Le Monde*, December 9 2017.

65 Stephen Lee Myers and Olivia Mitchell Ryan, "Once strict on births, China is scrambling to stimulate a Baby Boom", *The New York Times*, August 12, 2018.

The debate is open; soft here, better asserted elsewhere. It will grow in the coming years. The world is likely to see an increasing number of African governments, like Morocco's, that will set up ministries of population or public structures for analyses, proposals and interventions relating to population issues. These ministries will have to situate African demographic trends in the context of the overall population flows affecting humanity at the beginning of this twenty-first century. It is true that it may still be difficult for many to talk normally about Africa, but the colonial ink will eventually dry.

This progress must be seen in the light of the demographic evolution of humanity, which has increased threefold since 1950, from 2.5 billion five hundred million to 7.5 billion five hundred million, and twofold since 1970, from 3.7 billion seven hundred million to 7.5 billion five hundred million. These data put into perspective the "magnitude" of what is announced, i.e. the doubling of the number of Africans in the next thirty years.

Vast demographic movements are no stranger to the recent history of humanity. China's population has doubled in the last half-century, from 1960 to the present; India's population has tripled over the same period. The doubling of Africa's population is therefore not a first in the modern and contemporary era.

Admittedly, the projected demographic enrichment of the African continent, which in 2050 will include three of the ten most populous countries in the world, raises, here as elsewhere, the question of responsibility; that of individuals, families, social groups and religious and political leaders. However, it is only one component of the vast demographic movement affecting humanity in the twenty-first century.

The truth is, we will continue to be challenged by two opposing movements, two contrasting demographic trends that have begun to unfold simultaneously in our time.

In the West[66], the population of the United States will continue to grow modestly while in Russia, Germany, Japan, China and South Korea, demographic collapse threatens to weaken or even overturn the paradigms that have made these countries and regions the motors of economic growth and main global powers at various times. Thus, it is

---

66 This growth will not be enough, however, to spare Americans from the realities of an aging population. Read: E. Tammy Kim. "Who will care for you when you're old?" By 2050, about 80 million Americans will be senior citizens; nearly all will want to live at home. The country's 3 million aides are already overworked and underfunded. *Bloomberg Businessweek*, February 9, 2018.

expected that by 2050, the population of Germany will drop from 57 to 44 million, that of Italy from 43 million to 38, that of Spain and that of France will experience minor upward variations.

In China, the over-60 age group accounted for 12% of the population, or one hundred and sixty-six million people in 2000; it will represent 31% of the population, or four hundred and forty million people, by 2050. In South Asia and on the African continent, the demographic enrichment expected between now and 2050 reaches at least one billion births for each. This demographic enrichment will result in a doubling of the populations of these two great regions.

Contrasting trends, to say the least.

These changes in the human resource are rooted deep in ethical, cultural, economic and social systems; deep as well in the diverse histories and contrasting needs of the human family.

Africa belongs to these vast movements. It would be absurd to isolate it. Its demographic situation is as singular and complex as that of all other regions of the world. Africa, like all of them, has to manage it by taking into account regional and national variations. Some African countries have a higher ratio than four children per woman; others have a ratio of less than three children per woman. In Southern Africa, the density is ten people per square kilometre, forty-eight in Cameroon and 461 in Rwanda.

As a result, policies cannot be the same across the continent given these wide variations: relatively low in Southern Africa, average in West Africa and high in some Central African countries. The same policy for all these regions would be an absurdity.

Policies will also have to adjust to the continuous variations in forecasts due to multiple factors: accelerated urbanization and urban family size; increased school enrolment of adolescents, both girls and boys, which is expected to become widespread and compulsory until the age of 16; contraceptive and abortion laws; regulations relating to the age of marriage; female employment rates; public policies, including social and fiscal policies; regional, continental and international migration; and information and awareness-raising campaigns by Governments, national and international organizations, the media and civil society organizations.

This set of variations gives rise to very contrasting lessons. Some, relatively few in number, including the African editor of *The Economist*, use them to challenge United Nations projections of a doubling of the continent's population by the middle of the century.[67]

---

[67] Jonathan Rosenthal, "The-2.5-billion-persons question. Demographic projections for Africa could prove wildly wrong", *The Economist,* The World in 2019.

If humanity has been able to manage its doubling in the last forty years properly, it should be possible to do the same for the African continent in the next thirty years.

We must be wary of false news such as that which organically links population growth and poverty. According to a Brookings study, 42% of the world's population lived below the poverty line in 1991, as opposed to 10.7% in 2013. Never before have so many people been lifted out of poverty in such a short period of time, and that happened at the same time as the world's population grew by 59%. The Brookings researchers conclude that far from being a problem as once thought, population growth has gone hand in hand with increased prosperity. The increase in world population has meant an increase in world production.

Why shouldn't the same be true for Africa? Why not adopt development models that combine population growth and economic growth, the former invariably leading to a continuous increase in demand for goods and services, as has been the case in other regions of the world?

Finally, it is important to highlight our observations on African demographic dynamics with those concerning the expected evolution of the entire human family. If the median age was 26 at the beginning of the century, it will be 36 in 2050. By then, the people over sixty will be two billion, or 21% of humanity, compared with 625 million today. At that point in time, there will be four working people for every one pensioner in the so-called industrialized countries, compared with nine today. Of course, we may then be able to count on the brotherhood of robots, but there will still be many problems relating to savings, investment, consumption, the labour market, health, housing, pensions, lifestyles and living spaces. These issues are already the subject of public debate and challenge, particularly in Europe.

Might the question of migration be asked differently in view of the huge human resource needs that will be faced by the so-called industrialized countries, particularly in Europe?

Might the question of migration be asked differently in view of the immense needs for goods and services of the ageing populations of Western countries and certain Asian countries?

If we are on the threshold "of a new cycle of repopulation of the planet, migration will not stop. On the contrary, the earth is on the eve of new exoduses," in the words of Achilles Mbembe.

It is likely that the global demographic changes announced by some as "profound imbalances" will lead to a gradual change in the location of populations and a shift in the production of goods and services. We could then witness a second wave of industrial relocation, including scientific and technological research. Then, the demographic situation in Africa could appear to be part of the solution to the problems facing humanity much more than a large-scale disorder.

Already in 2012, the authors of the vast prospective study "Global Europe 2050" evoked the arrival in Europe of one million or even two million immigrants per year, depending on the scenarios adopted, i.e. a volume that could reach nearly one hundred million by the middle of the century.[68] Taking into account the declining trend in fertility rates on the continent, the International Monetary Fund (IMF) has set this volume at thirty four million by 2050. As Michel Agier, who opposes Stephen Smith's[69] alarmist theories, points out, Europe is not the only destination for African migrants. They emigrate and will emigrate first and foremost to their continent, in a majority, but also to Asia and the Americas.

These prospects should have an impact on the volume, consistency and quality of public and private, national and international investment on the continent in the medium term. They should also ultimately enrich intra-African trade and Africa's share of international trade in the first half of this century. This trinity is essential and vital.

In short, convergences are indispensable for the success of the announced African demographic enrichment: convergence between population, investments and technologies.

The successful convergence between demography and investment is one of the two foundations of the continent's growth and development in the 21st century. It concerns both the targeted use of Africans› own savings according to their priorities and international investment aimed at the development of the continent, particularly the development and maintenance of its tangible and intangible infrastructure. Ultimately, this arrangement, which is so similar to that which prevails elsewhere in the world, will allow the establishment of an economic and commercial ecosystem that places the operators of the continent in a dominant position in relation to all operations taking place on it. It will also allow the junction between these operations and the needs stemming from the growth of the continent›s population.

The second convergence concerns technology, one that is adapted to the climate, the needs and the financial possibilities of consumers, to a service offer, as is the case of India, capable of delivering to the masses and adapted to the multiple languages and cultures of Africans. A technology thought or rethought in relation to the needs of the continent.

---

68 European Commission, Global Europe, Research and Innovation, 2012.

69 Stephen Smith, « La ruée vers l'Europe », Paris, Grasset, 2018

This includes the work – plans, estimates, contracts and financing – required by the announced growth of the continent's current cities, a growth of around 100% by 2040. The resulting incompressible social needs, from food to housing, from health care to schooling for hundreds of millions of children who will, for the first time, be on the doorstep of schools between now and 2050, come to mind. There is also the absolute need to create millions of jobs year after year and to develop private and public services such as collective insurance, which accounts for 1% of today's GDP compared to the Latin American and Asian averages of 3% and 6% respectively. Finally, the logistical and material needs arising from the announced strong increase in land, sea and air traffic bear mention. None of these situations will find a lasting solution outside the continent, outside the African-led initiatives, outside the successful meeting of demography, investment and technology.

These vast projects will be carried out in particular by one of the rare young populations in the world, along with that of South Asia. A precious exception in a very ageing humanity. In the next twenty years, sub-Saharan Africa will see more people join the workforce than the rest of the world. In 2050, this labour force will total one billion six hundred million employable people, or 74% of the continent's total population. Life expectancy will then be seventy years for sub-Saharan Africans and eighty to eighty-three years for North Africans.

This unique positioning has been expressed in various ways: the largest reserve of labour on the planet; the next major destination for industrial relocation; the next manufacturing centre in the world where human labour will gradually be combined with that of robots powered by artificial intelligence; a market which, together with India, could be "the engine of world growth" in the coming decades.

An urbanized Africa

No forward-looking profile of Africa can avoid the predicted growth of the continent's cities, as it is and will remain decisive.

In an inexorable march that began two centuries ago, humanity has moved from rural territories, both tangible and intangible, to their urban counterparts. These movements are reaching their outcome in our time. In 1950, the world's urban population totalled 740 million people. A century later, 6.2 billion people will live in cities, an increase of 800%. Between 2000 and 2020, the number of cities with ten million or more inhabitants has doubled.

The great march was first that of the populations of the so-called developed countries followed, in recent decades, by the population of

China. In 2050, nine hundred and ten million Chinese nationals will live in cities compared to one hundred and seventy-two million in 1980. It is predicted that more than one hundred Chinese cities will have more than one million inhabitants by the middle of the century.

The populations of South Asia and Africa are currently closing the historic urbanization gap. In 2050, more than one billion one hundred million Indian nationals will live in cities, compared to sixty-two million in 1950. In 2050, one billion two hundred million Africans, or 56% of the continent's population, will live in cities compared to less than fifty million in 1950. The continent ranks first in terms of the pace of urban growth. It is the highest in the world.

Two thirds of new urban dwellers will be born or settle in existing cities and metropolises. The remaining one-third will be in the new cities emerging in Africa as well as in China and South Asia.[70] Before our eyes, the "millennium of cities" evoked by Kofi Annan is unfolding.

Some of the continent's cities will experience spectacular growth by the middle of the century. Kinshasa, Lagos and Cairo will have thirty-five, thirty-two and twenty-five million citizens respectively; eleven cities will have more than ten million; twenty-five others will have more than five million.

Today, on the continent, we stopped counting existing cities' new districts and even just new cities: Abuja and Eco Atlantic City in Nigeria; Ouaga-2000 and Yennega in Burkina Faso; Sidi Abdellah in Algeria, Oyala in Equatorial Guinea; Akwaba City in Côte d'Ivoire; Konza City in Kenya, Diamniadio Lake City in Senegal; Mohamed VI Tangier Tech where Huawei has just set up a regional logistics centre; Innovation City in Rwanda; a new capital in Egypt[71], among many others.

Africa is a continent where cities are being created. Some of them have the desire to join the list of technological relays that integrate the resources offered by existing technologies, including green technologies, and are also innovation incubators. Certain people on the continent mention the exemplary nature of the South Korean city of Songdo, often presented as the most intelligent city on the planet.

This accelerated transition to urban civilization concerns the entire continent. In the next thirty years, more than a billion Africans will be the actors involved. This vast movement is a powerful lever for economic development and growth. We are thinking of studies,

---

70 Montee Reel, "A burst of new cities", *Blomberg Businessweek*, November 5, 2018.

71 Jenna Le Bras, « En Égypte, des travaux pharaoniques pour bâtir une nouvelle capitale », *Le Monde*, March 7, 2018.

plans, specifications, contracts of all kinds, the equipment and materials required, public supply and private development to produce in sufficient quantities the goods and services that this new African urban clientele, which is already counted in the hundreds of millions, needs.

From health to food, from energy to education, from security to transportation, from public hygiene to sports facilities, from cultural and leisure activities, from housing to catering, including water supply; from financial to information technology services: the list of needs to be met is considerable.

These prospects include a part of the labour supply that the continent must absolutely provide for its citizens, especially its youngest citizens. Annually, ten million young Africans will seek to enter the labour market by the middle of the century. In Africa, as elsewhere in the world, this development of existing and new cities as a result of urban population growth is causing a dramatic increase in demand in all sectors of human activity.

Part of this development of existing and new cities will be based on the tangible and intangible heritage of African societies; another part will depend on continental, regional and national consultations and policies. However, on the continent as elsewhere, the city will contribute to the strengthening of the middle class and to the growth of its income. In China, as mentioned earlier, urbanization and income growth are inseparable.

These consultations have recently developed on the continent, although it is too early to assess their actual impact. At the regional level, these include consultations that have been conducted by the Association of Cities and Communities of the Economic and Monetary Community of Central Africa (CEMAC) and the Council of Territorial Communities, a consultative body of the West African Economic and Monetary Union (UEMOA) [72]; at the continental level, the Technical Committee of Local Authorities for Urban Development and Decentralization of the African Union and the Organization of United Cities and Local Governments of Africa (UCLGA).

Formed from the merger of three pre-existing associations, this organization, whose headquarters are in Rabat, brings together forty national associations of local authorities from all regions of Africa and two thousand cities with more than one hundred thousand inhabi-

---

72 This Council has the following three objectives: to involve regional authorities in the integration process in order to meet the challenges of globalisation; to promote a system of multi-level governance; and to take account of people's concerns.

tants.[73] It promotes the creation of national associations of local authorities, their autonomy and the need for their dialogue with central governments. Finally, it encourages the sharing of best practices among African local governments, particularly on the occasion of the Africities Summit to be held every three years, the eighth edition of which took place in Marrakech in 2018. Five thousand urban policy-makers participated in the Summit. Together with the United Nations Economic Commission for Africa (UNECA), it developed the Urban Agenda for Africa, aimed at bringing sustainable development and urbanization together.

So how will Africa and Africans benefit from the demographic and urban enrichment that will profoundly influence the continent's development in the coming decades?

---

73 The African Union of Local Authorities (AULA), the Union of African Towns (UVA) and the African Chapter of the Portuguese-speaking Organization of Local Authorities (UCCLA).

Chapter Two

CREATING WEALTH FOR AND BY AFRICANS

The strong demographic and urban dynamics identified are inextricably linked to an economic trend on the same scale. This underlying economic impetus is underway, as evidenced notably by the range of business partnerships benefiting the continent. Admittedly, the convergences that support this economic trend could become distorted under the influence of a major crisis in the world economy. Yet, these unfinished convergences remain driven by powerful, complementary and sustainable flows.

Among these are emerging economic partnerships, particularly in Asia, in addition to the traditional relations between countries on the continent. Such partnerships have enriched perceptions of Africa as a growing market.

The profound and gradual transformation of the continent's economy is also being considered, as demonstrated, among other things, by the ongoing banking revival, the advances of the continent's stock markets, and the continuous increase in demand due to the ever-growing needs generated by demographic enrichment and urban development. These needs are well known: the growth of existing cities and the creation of new ones; unprecedented infrastructure development, particularly in the areas of land, air and sea transport; and the gradual appropriation by Africans of digital technologies and their many variations.

These developments are made possible as a result of Africans' slow and gradual takeover of their economic levers, as well as investments and support from Asian powers, particularly China and India.

Reference is also made to the favourable evolution of intra-African trade when it comes to wealth creation across the continent. As noted earlier, the volume of intra-African commerce has more than doubled since 2000 and now accounts for 18% of the continental trading.

Finally, the gradual development of hybrid industrialisation on the continent is conceivable as a significant factor, combining traditional systems, advanced forms of production of goods and services and the deployment of value chains including the transformation of basic materials and hitherto timid use of the levers offered by robotics and artificial intelligence. The convergence of these elements is real and powerful. It is emerging in several countries of the continent, including the ten that, according to the Africa CEO Forum, will have a growth rate of more than 6% between 2018 and 2030.[74]

Progressively, the continent is being carried along by the current that has been redrawing the financial, economic and commercial map of the world for a quarter of a century. It too is benefiting, albeit with some delay, from the wealth shift from the West to the Eastern and Southern parts of the world.

Africa is undergoing progressive breakthroughs, the convergence of which is gradually moving it away from the dependency that has profoundly affected it over half a century. The time of "deep and rapid transformation of the continent" desired by Dr. Amoakale, president of the African Center for Economic Transformation in Accra is approaching. It emerges from the very long period of dependence and subjugation that was its destiny in the modern and contemporary, pre- and post-independence, period.

New economic partners

The continent boasts new financial, economic and trading partners, especially in Asia, who regard it both as a growing solvent market and as a reservoir of natural resources.[75] This duality of perspectives has never been present in Europe's vision of Africa, a vision that imposed itself on the world in the modern period and much of the contempo-

---

74 Ethiopia, 8%; Rwanda and Mozambique, 7.5%; Côte d'Ivoire, Sierra Leone, Senegal, Tanzania, 6.5% and Uganda, Kenya and Burkina Faso, 6.2%. Euromonitor International

75 See the works of the South Africa Institute of International Affairs. www.saiia.org.za

rary period just like the one that is being developed by Asian countries is imposing itself today.

For the first time, the continent is benefiting from favourable conditions. It benefits from Chinese and Indian tariffs that are substantially lower than those in the West and also from patient capital that it has lacked over the last half-century. This capital is transforming the continent's economic fundamentals, as shown by the high volume of national, regional and continental infrastructure development completed or under way. These developments concern the development of means of ground transportation, roads and railways, including the Mombasa-Nairobi, Djibouti-Addis Ababa and Abuja-Kaduna railway lines. This involves the upgrading of air transportation and port facilities and the creation of new ports, which we will survey in more detail. It also concerns traditional energy production, such as hydroelectricity and the production of renewable energies such as solar and wind power.

In addition to these external resources, the continent is experiencing unprecedented experiences of pooling its internal reserves, such as the cooperation between six West African microcredit networks, which led to the creation of a sub-regional bank, the *Financière de l'Afrique de l'Ouest* (FINAO). Like the other banking groups which are at last in the hands of Africans, FINAO will take into account the need for longer-term credit, which until now has been difficult to obtain in the region and on the continent.[76]

With regard to urban development, United Cities and Local Governments of Africa (UCLGA) reminds us of the Addis Ababa Plan of Action of June 2015. This plan proposes the mobilization of domestic resources in order to feed an African Cities Development Fund. This Cooperative Development Fund is currently being set up. According to the Secretary General of the UCLGA, "local governments in Africa have immense margins of progress, largely untapped so far."[77]

Gradually, Africa is becoming a strategic link in global financial and trade policy. It is becoming a crossroads for all powers, no longer as a result of its dominance and the terrible systemic weaknesses that have resulted from it, but as a function of what it has to contribute and offer, which is substantial.[78]

---

76 Nadouin Coulibaly, « Microfinance, Des ressources pérennes et moins coûteuses », *Jeune Afrique*, no. 2989, 22 April–5 May 2018.

77 Jean-Pierre Elong-Mbassi, « Nous devons inventer un nouveau monde », *Afrique Magazine*, 383-384 – August-September 2018.

78 To appreciate more fully that African trajectory, one must read Jean Tabi Manga's important work « Des voix…: à la voie du temps. Variations sur la

The Europeans and Americans intend to maintain their presence in the region, while the Russians are trying to regain access, as illustrated in particular by the holding of a Russia-Africa Economic Forum held recently in October 2019 and an initiative to support investment.[79] Nevertheless, other financial, industrial and commercial systems are now deploying their capacities, logistical chains and brands in the area.

Arab partners

In the Arab world, those systems are increasingly involved through the work and decisions of the Arab-African Summit, the fourth edition of which was held in Malabo in November 2016; also through trade between the Emirates and the continent, which showcased a growth of more than 700% between 2008 and 2018; finally, through the facilities of the systems of some emirates, including Dubai, where a very large number of Africans and seventeen thousand companies from the continent are based.[80]

In an interview with Financial Afrik, the president of the Dubai Chamber of Commerce stated that "trade between his country and Africa in non-oil products reached more than one hundred and ninety-one billion dollars between 2013 and 2018".[81] In short, Islamic finance, whose assets are valued at four trillion dollars, is henceforth within the reach of African parties, companies and governments.

The channels for these investments are numerous: the Islamic Development Bank, which has notably invested in the agricultural sector[82]; the Saudi Fund, the Kuwait Fund, the OPEC Fund, the Arab Fund for Economic and Social Development, and others. These funds have all been active on the continent for two decades. Unlike Western lenders and according to formulas quite similar to those adopted by China to penetrate the continent, these funds "grant concessional credits at very low interest rates and over long terms."[83]

Renaissance, l'Émergence et la modernité africaines », Éditions OPECAM, Yaounde, 2014,

79 African business initiative (ABI), *La lettre du continent*, no 789, November 28 2018.

80 Christophe Le Bec, « Comment Dubaï est devenu un tremplin pour l'Afrique », *Jeune Afrique*, no 2984, du 18 au 24 mars 2018.

81 Entretien exclusif avec S.E. Hamad Buamim, President & CEO at Dubai Chamber of Commerce & Industry, September 7 2018.

82 As an example, the Islamic Development Bank is releasing 34.6 billion CFA francs to "boost" agriculture in Cameroon.

83 Ismail Omar Guelleh, Djibouti est libre de ses choix! Interview by Zyad Liman, *Afrique Magazine*, 377, February 2018.

Meanwhile, the (Arabic-speaking) countries of North Africa have multiple economic ties with the countries south of the Sahara. There was a time, not so long ago, when Algeria was at the forefront of this ancient and current relationship, while Morocco and Tunisia engaged as well in significant cooperation.

At present, Morocco, whose economy doubled in size between 2000 and 2012, has firmly established itself at the forefront of this relationship between the continent's two geographical components, Africa north and Africa south of the Sahara. With a determined, voluntarist and continuous policy, the kingdom is extending its financial, economic and industrial networks on the continent. In terms of investment, it has even surpassed France, whose market share has collapsed between 2005 and 2015, from 7% to 4%.[84]

A quarter of the world's Muslims are African, while more than 50%, by the middle of this century, will be African. It is not unusual for financiers and financial institutions of this cultural movement to take an interest in the continent's affairs, particularly in the primary sectors of education, health, energy, industrialization and technology. It now seems profitable for African governments to issue bonds to this market (Islamic bonds) as the governments of Nigeria, Senegal and Côte d'Ivoire, among others, have done.

Morocco: an African power

This new dynamism of the South-South economic relationship, in terms of investment and trade, is also taking place within the continent itself, as can be seen in Morocco's multidimensional action in Africa.[85]

The second largest African investor on the continent after South Africa, Morocco, deploys capital, technology, logistical and management systems in more than twenty countries across the continent. The Kingdom's trade with the continent grew by 11%, on average annually, between 2005 and 2015, a threefold increase to reach nearly 4.5 billion dollars in 2016. Companies in the banking, telephony and insurance sectors account for 85% of these investments and offer their services throughout the CFA area and beyond. For their part, Moroccan banks control a third of the market on the sub-continent. Their presence there is clear.

84 « Une puissante diaspora », *Afrique Magazine*, February 2018.

85 Other examples could have been selected from institutions and companies from Nigeria, Mozambique, South Africa, Egypt, Mauritius and others that have invested on the continent.

For instance, in 2018, the Attijariwafa bank had four hundred and forty-three points of service in the zone, a superb network for its subsidiary WAFA Insurance. Itisalat-al-Maghreb, Morocco's largest telecom company derives 43% of its profits from its affiliated divisions in the region.[86] Lastly, the OVP group, the powerful Moroccan phosphate company, has created a subsidiary with the ambition of multiplying its sales by five by 2025. Adapted products, on-site processing, storage close to customers and local product marketing: the ambition, in time, is to build production plants in Sub-Saharan Africa.[87]

This renewed dynamism in South-South economic relations is also illustrated by the progressive deployment of African goods and services companies, from their countries of origin to their regions and the continent.[88]

Taking support from communication technologies, these various movements are gradually linking the continent to universal technological systems. Africans have adopted them with obvious interest. More than 700 million Africans have smartphones; more than 500 million have access to the Internet; and in two decades over one billion will. The technology transfer from the world to the continent, and from some countries of the continent to other African countries, is too limited but finally unlocked. It is served by this set of converging movements which, through investment now coming from multiple sources, are moving Africa and Africans forward.

Morocco and North Africa more broadly have been positioned as significant on the world map of aeronautics and automobile production[89]; Ethiopia on the map of mobile phones and clothing production; South Africa on the map of pharmaceutical production; Kenya,

86 "Morocco's new friends, Making eyes across the Sahara", *The Economist*, July 21, 2018.

87 Christophe Le Bec, « Le groupe OCP revoit sa stratégie en Afrique subsaharienne », *Jeune Afrique*, March 6-12 2016.

88 Morocco's relationship with the continent has also been enriched in recent years by major political initiatives, including the Kingdom's return to the AU and its intention to join ECOWAS. It has also been enriched by cooperation initiatives. These include debt cancellation for the least developed countries of the continent, Rabat's participation in peacekeeping operations, the regularization of irregular sub-Saharan Africans, the increase in the number of scholarships and the training of imams.

89 The following Chinese companies are established or have announced new facilities in North African countries: Byd in Morocco, Beijing Automobile International Corporation (BAIC) and Chery in Algeria, Dongfeng in Tunisia and SAIC Motors in Egypt.

Rwanda and Côte d'Ivoire on the map of opportunities offered by the Financial Services Network, to name just a few.

There is something of a paradigm shift in Africa with regard to development and growth. Must we see in that the existence of development and growth models other than the Western model, models that have clearly been successful? It is perhaps that these models are better suited to the formidable stakes and challenges that Africans must address in a meaningful way in the coming decades.

As we said earlier, if Europeans and Americans strive to remain on the continent and Russians try to re-enter its market, other financial, industrial and commercial systems will deploy their capabilities, their supply chains and their brands throughout. While partnerships with the Arab world are important, those with the Asian countries deserve to be pointed out.

The Asian partners

In various capacities, many Asian countries now place Africa within the scope of their global interests. One need only visit the continent's major industrial parks[90] to see Korean, Japanese, Chinese, Vietnamese, Indian and Indonesian brands and, in the ports, goods from these countries but also from Thailand, Malaysia and Singapore.

Indifferent to the continent just a few years ago, the government of Singapore, through Enterprise Singapore, its secular arm in charge of overseas investment and trade, recently multiplied its representative offices on the continent, in Ghana, Kenya, South Africa, etc., to support the impact of its companies which already operate in fifty countries of the continent.

In addition to the major contributions of the Asian governments, in particular India and China, the latter being the leading trading partner and the main source of investment on the continent, the private sector companies of these countries are also stakeholders in this formidable mooring between the two continents.

We think of many public and private Chinese companies, with large amounts of their own resources and considerable lines of credit. Until recently absent from the continent, they are now active in a large number of these countries, opening branches such as the one recently opened in Senegal by the Chinese Machinery Engineering Corporation (CMEC).

---

90 According to the Ethiopian Growth and Transformation Plan 2015-2020, twenty of these parks were to be open by 2020.

There are also large Indian companies that, in some cases, have been operating in Africa for more than half a century: Tata,[91] Mahindra,[92] Arcelor Mittal,[93] Rambaxy,[94] Bharti Airtel, the second largest mobile phone operator on the continent with operations in fifteen countries, Oil India Limited, M3M India, Ramky Engineering and Consulting Services.[95] According to studies conducted at the Harvard Business School, multinationals in emerging countries "are growing twice as fast as companies in developed countries, both in their domestic markets and abroad."[96]

In 2016, 28% of new foreign direct investment in Africa came from companies in emerging countries compared to 8% in 2000. In the same year, the top ten investors in Africa by number of major projects included China, India, Kenya and South Africa.[97]

China as a partner

A race between the two Asian giants is taking shape on the African continent. China is currently its largest trading partner, its largest source of investment and its leading job creator.[98] It is the only country to rank among the continent's leading partners in terms of trade, the value of foreign direct investment, infrastructure financing and official development assistance.[99] It is said to have invested close to two hundred billion dollars between 2006 and 2016, 10% of which would have been allocated to the manufacturing sector.

For the continent, China is also a major trading partner. Indeed, since the beginning of the century, Sino-African trade has increased twenty-fold. In 2017, the total volume of China's imports and exports with Africa totalled one hundred and seventy billion dollars, including imports of African products to the tune of seventy billion dollars, the rest representing Chinese exports to the continent.

---

91 Steel, telecommunications and hospitality industries.

92 Agricultural equipment.

93 Steel industry.

94 Generic drugs.

95 Telecommunications.

96 HBR, *op. cit.*

97 "South-to-South Investment, Developing Ties", *The Economist*, February 10, 2018.

98 FDI Markets, The Africa Report 2017.

99 Aboubacar Yacouba Barma, « Chine-Afrique: un partenariat largement sous-estimé selon McKinsey », *La Tribune Afrique*, June 29 2017.

The Chinese imprint is everywhere. It is in the infrastructures: railways, stadiums, airports, ports, highways, congress centres, cultural centres, etc. A considerable proportion of the continent's modern infrastructure bears this signature. It is in the production of goods, from mines to clothing production; from energy to agriculture, etc. It is also in the production of services: the education system, including the grandes écoles, the environment, health, leisure, culture, etc.

In 2016, the consulting firm McKinsey Africa released a study whose content contrasts with many opinions on the nature, dimensions and consequences of the China-Africa relationship. It estimated the number of Chinese companies active on the continent at ten thousand, 90% of which are private companies. One thousand of them were interviewed for that study.[100]

The experts of the consulting firm are categorical. In their appreciation, the Chinese presence in Africa has greatly contributed to the dynamism of the continent's economy, including job creation and transfer of knowledge and technology. This has obviously contributed to the enrichment of Chinese companies which, according to the same report, have declared profits of 20% in 2015, hence their optimism. Indeed, 75% of them have a positive assessment of the continent's potential. This quasi balance sheet is impressive and is positively appreciated by those in Africa and elsewhere in the world who share the opinion of philosopher Bashir Diagne: "Africa has nothing to fear from China."

But how did China and Africa come together?

Barely out of a long period of internal difficulties, from the cultural revolution to the debate on the transformation of the country's economy and the first steps of this impossible yet successful transformation in just a few short years, the Chinese authorities have made an inventory of world affairs and their place in that world. They then agreed that their ongoing success cannot be confined within their national borders. Hence the policy adopted in 1996 of "Going out to the world" and the decisive choice of Africa as a priority area for China's international expansion.

Initiated in the 1990s and implemented in the 2000s, this internationalization strategy for companies aims to secure their access to natural resources.[101] The parameters of this policy have, as of 2010,

100 According to the Study, 89% of the employees surveyed were African, representing nearly 300,000 jobs. "On the scale of all 10,000 Chinese companies in Africa, this suggests that Chinese companies employ several million Africans".

101 « Le soutien public à l'internationalisation des entreprises chinoises. Bulletin économique de Chine », Publications des services du Trésor, no.79, November-December 2015.

integrated the construction of infrastructures in targeted countries using equipment and materials produced in China in sectors with overcapacity. In this "Going out" policy, Africa occupies a prominent place for economic as well as politico-strategic reasons.

In economic terms, China has been Africa's largest trading partner since 2009. In order to sustain its long-term growth, it has an incompressible need for the quantities of raw materials and fossil resources it finds on the African continent. It also needs them as a major and continuously growing market.

At the politico-strategic level, Africa allows China to consolidate its international stature and to settle various issues, including its strategic competition with Taiwan. It is increasing its influence at the United Nations and nurturing its ambition to reconfigure the international chessboard.[102] The rhetoric used by Chinese Prime Minister Li Keqiang during his long African tour in 2014 is better understood with all that in mind. Our relations, he then said in the capitals of Ethiopia, Nigeria and Angola, have entered "a golden age".

It is therefore an "easy mistake", according to Howard French, to limit China's interest in Africa to the continent's natural resources alone. Admittedly, they are of great importance to China, which urgently needs them for the construction of its infrastructure and the development of its urban areas, which are constantly growing. However, they are part of a broader intention. Indeed, if American investments in Africa are concentrated at the level of 62% in the mining sector, those of the Chinese are much more diversified, the mining sector representing only 28% of their total investments on the continent.[103]

The second pillar of Beijing's Africa policy concerns the international purpose of the presence of Chinese companies in Africa. This presence is thought of and deployed as a step in the conquest of the global market, in the establishment of these companies as "global players".

Finally, the third pillar of China's strategy concerns the bet it took in relation to the emergence by the middle of the century of a vibrant African middle class, abundantly consuming goods and services. There is a Chinese dream of Africa that combines the interests of both parties, according to French.

---

102 Laurence Daziano, « Pourquoi les États-Unis sont devancés par la Chine en Afrique? », August 8 2014.

103 David Pilling, "Beijing's push into Africa is shifting the axis of an entire continent", *Financial Times*, June 14, 2017.

In order to durably win over Africa, Beijing needs three major operations to be successful. The first is to maintain and increase its own investment flows and raise its contribution to the various mechanisms set up with African partners such as the China-Africa Development Fund to a high level. Secondly, Beijing must maintain the participation of the countries of the continent in its major cooperation ventures such as the Silk Road. To Ethiopia, Djibouti, South Africa and Morocco, which were the gateways to the continent, the Chinese authorities have just added West Africa on the occasion of the Forum on Sino-African Cooperation in September 2018. Finally, Beijing must implement its plan to industrialize the continent by relocating manufacturing production that no longer meets the conditions of the labour market in China, increase its investment in agriculture as the transition from subsistence to industrialization and agro-industry meets urgent needs and will have a positive impact, here as elsewhere, on economic growth. All these projects must give access to global production chains controlled by China and be extended into the digital space.

These objectives can be broken down into multiple areas, from training to job creation, from technology transfer to the creation of laboratories of the future on the continent capable of creating science and its applications, supporting innovation and contributing to a scientific culture specific to the continent in view of its specific characteristics. These objectives are being pursued through investment by Chinese companies. Huawei, for example, trains more than 12,000 students in its centres in Angola, the Congo, Egypt, Morocco, Nigeria and South Africa.[104] These goals are also implemented in the large industrial parks created by China in Africa, including Ethiopia, Djibouti and Morocco, with the Mohammed VI Cité announcing 100,000 jobs. This rapprochement is undoubtedly enriched by the holding of the Year of Morocco in China in 2020.

The Indian partner

The great Asian democracy does not yet have a presence on the continent comparable to that of China. However, according to journalist Walid Kefi, "if the Indian elephant is not yet running as fast as the Chinese dragon flies, it is still determined to cross the finish line near the top."[105]

---

104 David Pilling, *op. cit.*

105 Walid Kéfi, « Pour l'Inde, se rapprocher de l'Afrique devient une affaire d'état », *Ecofin Hebdo*, April 6 2018.

A series of recent political decisions made by the Indian government underpin this assertion: the India-Africa summit held every three years, repeated visits by the Indian President and Prime Minister to the continent, eighteen new Indian embassies to be opened in Africa between 2018 and 2022, in addition to the twenty-nine existing diplomatic missions.

These political commitments are accompanied by a range of important economic proposals: a free trade agreement between India and Africa; the creation of an India-Africa Development Fund with an initial capital of ten billion dollars, the extension of credits from the Indian Export-Import Bank to almost all the countries of the continent, and high-level financial support for more than twenty major solar energy projects.

Finally, in this multifaceted approach, several elements of which resemble Chinese tools for penetrating the continent, India has recently joined Japan in a gigantic project: the Asia-Africa Growth Corridor also known as the Freedom Corridor. This road is intended to be a real alternative to the major Chinese Silk Road programme. The competition is set to be fierce.

The two projects are described by a New Delhi diplomat as follows: "Unlike the Chinese initiative, the Indian initiative is a model of fair, transparent and mutually beneficial cooperation in terms of growth and connectivity. Moreover, this project does not violate the sovereignty of any country".[106] A word to the wise.

This set of levers has already produced significant results, including the desired increase in India-Africa trade. They amounted to 11.9 billion dollars in 2005, 49 billion dollars ten years later and the target for 2022 has been set at 150 billion dollars. India is the continent's second largest trading partner, ahead of the United States and France.

The Indian diaspora on the continent is significant. It is made up of three million people with ancient roots in Africa. The map of Indian investment on the continent partly overlaps with that of its diaspora, from Mauritius to Kenya, South Africa to Uganda. Indians have also chosen to invest in Egypt, Mozambique, Sudan, Tunisia, Ethiopia and Senegal, among others. The Delhi-Rabat cooperation is in gestation and could bring major investments to the kingdom. It finally took shape at the beginning of 2019, following the signing of four cooperation agreements between India and Morocco covering the fields of housing, urban policy and the intelligent city, youth, security and the issuing of business visas.

---

106 *Ibid.*

The American partner

It appears, as previously stated, that the Americans are trying to return to a continent in which, incidentally, its oil multinationals have maintained a long-standing presence. Exxon Mobil, to take but one example, has recently moved into the Angolan Basin to complement its investments in Mauritania, Nigeria, Chad, Angola, Namibia, South Africa and Tanzania. The apparent disinterest of the Americans was not equally shared.

Heading into 2019, a number of American companies appear to have renewed their appetite for the continent beyond the energy and natural resources sectors. In November 2018, the *Lettre du Continent* was titled: "Investment funds storm the innovation market." This storming of the new technologies' markets will be further detailed below.

In October 2018, the President of the United States signed the Better Utilization of Investments Leading to Development – BUILD – Act. A new U.S. federal agency was born, the U.S. International Development Finance Corporation. With a budget of 60 billion dollars, the mission of this new agency is to offer new financial products for private sector companies wishing to invest in what the American government still calls "the developing world". The agency will be responsible for the development of new financial products for the private sector. This BUILD Act is said to be designed to take on China in Africa.

At the end of 2018, on a reconnection mission to Côte d'Ivoire and leading a delegation to assess investment opportunities, the U.S. Under Secretary of Commerce said U.S. government agencies and private companies plan to invest \$4.5 billion in four countries on the continent, Ghana, Kenya, Côte d'Ivoire and Ethiopia. The official also said the U.S. Trade and Development Agency (USTDA) will expand its work on the continent to help increase trade between America and Africa. In early 2019, the Brooking Institute published a major report on the opportunities offered by Africa to American investors presented as "the world's next big growth market".[107]

Laudable, these initiatives still appear modest in relation to America's public and private investment capacities, in relation to the continent's possibilities and needs, and relative to the competition,

---

[107] Acha Leke et Landry Signé, "Spotlighting opportunities for business in Africa and strategies to succeed in the world's next big growth market", *Brooking Institute*, January 11, 2019.

particularly from Asia. Furthermore, they lack political packaging, a perspective that is, as it is for China and, to a lesser degree for India, the promise of an effective partnership in the long term.

Finally, some Latin American countries, including Brazil, Chile and Mexico, have shown interest in the continent and have made certain investments. A more favourable political and economic climate could no doubt revive what appears to be a real but unfulfilled intention.

The European partner

The twenty-year Cotonou Agreement, concluded in 2000, follows the arcana of the historic agreements between the European Union (EU) and the group of seventy-nine ACP countries (Sub-Saharan Africa, Caribbean, Pacific). It is more a reflection of the colonial past than of the requirements of cooperation illuminating the first century of the third millennium. It is so in its spirit, which gives pride of place to the outdated North-South dichotomy. It is so in its management, which is said to be cumbersome and complex, so cumbersome and complex that the sums allocated are not fully committed and spent by the parties. The European Development Fund (EDF), which is responsible for implementing this policy, is harshly judged and has suffered a 15% reduction in its budgets in recent years.

Political conditions, conflict prevention and resolution, migration management: the project framework is tight and managed ambitiously. Many Africans feel that the signed agreements constitute de facto parameters set unilaterally by the European parties. To put it simply, these agreements are a legacy of what is desired, namely the development of the economy through investment, the transfer and sharing of technology, the effective development of infrastructure, support for African production of goods and services and access to the potential of digital technology. This last item appears only marginally in this framework of another time. In short, several African leaders who find more advantageous partnerships elsewhere severely criticize the spirit of their relationship and understanding with the European Union.

Between the parties, a long period of research was necessary in order to relaunch their relationship on a new basis. EU-Africa Summits have been held; the European Commission tabled a strategy for Africa in 2005, followed by an action plan in 2008. The results are not convincing. It is necessary to do differently, according to officials on both sides. Formulas that are better adapted to needs and time are being sought and developed.

Among these are the EU-Africa partnership to strengthen African peacekeeping capabilities; the Mediterranean Transgreen and Desertec projects in the energy sector; and the financing of infrastructure for which the tenth EDF has set aside more than 8 billion dollars. However, as evidenced by the strong controversy surrounding the Economic Partnership Agreements (EPAs), which Africans have strongly opposed, it appears that a number of issues have not been fully resolved. In their view, these EPAs, genuine free trade agreements, replaced a system of non-reciprocal trade that was favourable to them. In the state of development of African economies, the abandonment of this system seemed suicidal. As a result, the majority of African states rejected the EPAs.

Each party is now more flexible in its positions. The EU has taken note of the massive presence of other powers on the continent and the Africans, who are in a better negotiating position, are not unhappy to use Europeans as a counterweight to the Chinese presence in particular. The magic spell is still needed to reshape the framework of Europe's relationship with Africa. In 2017, at the summit bringing together the African Union and the European Union, the President of the European Commission, Jean-Claude Juncker, said the essential point: "What happens in Africa matters to Europe, and what happens in Europe matters to Africa. »

An economy in the making

This reconfiguration of the continent's external economic relations has been accompanied by a considerable transformation of its own economy, as highlighted by the renewal of its banking system, the expansion of its stock exchanges, the deployment of the digital economy and the emergence of a private sector in continuous growth. As the colonial economic architecture dissipates, an economy specific to the continent is rising. Admittedly, it is far from complete and its development will be long and complex. However, this system exists and its progressive deployment is verifiable. Its consolidation will have multiple effects, including the transformation of political governance, which is now fiduciary to African interests much more than to external interests.

A Banking Renewal

Among the changes that positively mark the continent's progress and are likely to contribute to the creation of wealth in Africa, those that are affecting the financial, stock[108] market and banking configuration (financial services to companies and individuals) are of great importance. It is, in fact, a normalization because it seems abnormal that citizens, companies, various associations, local, regional and national governments have depended so much on branches of foreign institutions. The latter have been insensitive to their needs and unwilling to support the development of the local or national economy.

Until recently, this was the situation on the continent; a dependency on vast financial and industrial complexes which, from the metropolises, dominated the continent's profitable sectors and directed them according to their interests. This is now changing.

It is certainly not a question of closing the borders to all the institutions in the field, but, as all the countries of the world do, of establishing their functions and missions, which are complementary to those of the national, regional or continental system, without which the economy is dramatically extroverted.

The movements underway on the continent are moving in this direction. As we have noted, African banking institutions are asserting themselves in many ways.

They are entering into agreements with each other, such as the partnership signed in early 2018 between the pan-African EcoBank, which operates in thirty-three African countries, and South Africa's Nedbank; and the partnership signed in April 2018 between Nigeria's EcoBank Group and South African giant MTN, each of which makes their services available to their clients and to unbanked individuals.

They are asserting themselves by deploying their services throughout the continent. Among these are the branch facilities of major Moroccan banks such as Attijariwafa Bank and BMCE Bank which have branches in more than twenty countries on the continent and, in some of these countries, the creation of subsidiaries such as Wafa Credit that together with the Société ivoirienne des Banques serves the eight countries of the West African Economic and Monetary Union.

They are also asserting themselves by taking over the operations and clientele of foreign banks. These include the resumption of the activities of the French Banque Populaire and Caisse d'Epargne (BPCE) as "reference shareholders" in banking institutions in five countries on the continent, namely Madagascar, Mauritius, Tunisia,

108 Treasury bond emissions that can be linked to Treasury bonds have multiplied in recent years with a definite success. These appeals to investors in a country, sub-region or region-individuals, companies, banks have often produced coverage rates of more than 100%.

Cameroon and Congo-Brazzaville; the withdrawal of PNP Paribas from 50% of the shares held in the Gabonese Banque Internationale pour le Commerce et l'Industrie; and the sale by Barclays of its Egyptian subsidiary to the Moroccan company Attijariwafa.

In short, major European banks, which had dominated the field throughout the last century, are withdrawing from the continent in favour of "local entrepreneurs in the banking sector. »

They are asserting themselves by relying on mobile phone systems to offer services of all kinds, thereby recruiting customers and building networks that rank among the very best in the world.

In parallel, it should be noted that Asian banks, notably Chinese banks, have established themselves in Africa.[109] By acquiring 20% of South African Standard Bank, which operates in seventeen African countries, for USD 5.5 billion in 2011, the Industrial and Commercial Bank of China has consolidated its position on the continent and paved the way for its domestic competitors interested in the African market.

Much still remains to be done, however. As Frédéric Maury points out: "No banking sector in the world is as outrageously dominated by foreign players as retail banking in sub-Saharan Africa."[110] As a result, access to credit is severely limited where «local banks are more willing to take risks, innovate and lend.»[111] This limitation affects all sectors, including trade finance, whose deficit in 2016, according to the International Chamber of Commerce, totalled $1.6 billion.

The ongoing standardization should ensure the collection, management and investment of African savings by institutions owned by Africans based on analyses and recommendations made in Africa by African experts. Ultimately, it should produce a range of financial products adapted to the needs and capacities of the continent's economies, including the necessary patient capital margins.

In addition, this standardization should facilitate participation in national, regional and continental financial syndicates and national and continental funds dedicated to investment. [112] This includes the

---

109 Two Chinese banks have become very well known on the African continent. They finance major public projects decided by governments. They are the Development Bank of China, which is the largest development institution in the world with much more capital than the World Bank, and the Export-Import Bank of China.

110 Frédéric Maury, Édito, « L'opportunité nationale », *Jeune Afrique*, no 2970, December 10-16 2017.

111 Idem.

112 Rwanda Innovation Fund.

African Solidarity Fund (ASF) dedicated to guaranteeing and refinancing loans. Based in Niamey since its creation in 1976, this fund has an authorized capital of one hundred and fifty billion FCFA but is still awaiting its full development.[113] Another example is the African Guarantee and Economic Cooperation Fund (FAGACE). Dedicated to the promotion of investment, this Fund headquartered in Kigali has a capital of three hundred and fifty billion CFA francs in 2015.[114]

Numerous funds have been set up by the AfDB: the African Guarantee Fund (AGF) based in Arusha, Tanzania, whose mission is to facilitate access to financing for SMEs and SMIs; the Africa 50 Fund, which enjoys the support of 30 countries, has a capital of US$ 850 million and is designed to support infrastructure projects in regional economic communities, urban communities and cities.[115] Created in 2015 by the AfDB and domiciled in Casablanca, Africa 50 is a legally and financially independent entity dedicated to infrastructure financing.

For many, the ongoing standardization process should lead to the abandonment of the CFA franc for the so-called French-speaking zone of the continent and, eventually, the replacement of the IMF by an African Monetary Fund.[116]

Finally, African-majority consortia of financial institutions such as the Forum of Clubs of Bank Managers of the continent should advocate for the continent's interests in international organizations in the field, including the powerful Bank for International Settlements (BIS).

Apart from the Central Bank of South Africa, no bank in sub-Saharan Africa is a member of the powerful Bank for International Settlements in Basel. Its decisions have a direct impact on the rules

---

113 The fourteen member states are Benin, Burkina Faso, Chad, Côte d'Ivoire, Guinea Bissau, Mali, Niger, Senegal, Togo, Gabon, CAR, Burundi, Mauritius and Rwanda.

114 The Member States are the same as for the FCFA: Cameroon, Congo-Brazzaville, Mauritania instead of Gabon and Burundi.

115 In March 2018, the Urban Community of Douala raised CFAF 10 billion to enable its investment company to carry out major projects; Douala International Conference Centre, Multimodal Station, Exhibition Centre, etc.

116 Kako Nubupko (dir), Martial Ze Belinga, Bruno Tinel, Demba Moussa Dembele, « Sortir l'Afrique de la servitude monétaire. À qui profite le franc CFA? » Paris, L*a Dispute*, 2016

Gabriel Fal, « Pour sortir du franc CFA, OPTONS POUR UN Fonds monétaire africain », *Jeune Afrique*, no 2980, February 18-24 2018.

Michel Santi, « Francs CFA, clef voûte de la Françafrique », *La tribune*, February 14 2019.

applicable to all the world's commercial banks, including the rules for lending to individuals and companies. Do these decisions take into account the particular situation of the continent's economies and the needs of Africans?

Emerging Stock Exchanges

Long dominated by foreign institutions, Africa's financial system is gradually integrating financial markets that are normalizing and bringing the continent's financial system closer to those prevailing elsewhere in the world.

The continent's financial markets were formed late, as colonization left no room for African financial institutions. In so doing, it severely constrained overall economic development, deprived African governments of first-generation bond resources, and blocked the formation and growth of a private sector. In terms of capitalization, the chronological backwardness of the continent is considerable, the stock exchanges of New York, Tokyo, Sao Paulo, Hong Kong and Mexico City having been created in 1817, 1878, 1890, 1891 and 1933 respectively. Even older, those of Amsterdam, Paris, London and Brussels date from 1611, 1639, 1698 and 1801 respectively. Only a handful of stock exchanges on the continent were established during the colonial period: the Johannesburg Stock Exchange (JSE) in 1887; the Alexandria and Cairo Stock Exchanges, now merged, in 1883 and 1903 respectively, and the Casablanca Stock Exchange in 1929.[117]

All the other African financial markets have more or less followed the timetable of the independence movement, that of English-speaking Africa preceding that of French-speaking Africa: 1954 for Nairobi and 1960 for Nigeria; 1969 for the Tunis Stock Exchange, 1998 for the Abidjan Regional Stock Exchange and 2003 for the Libreville Stock Exchange.

The vast majority of the twenty-seven existing African stock exchanges have been established over the last thirty years. The arrival is late, the deployment is slow, but the progress in progress is significant.[118]

Private capital flows to sub-Saharan Africa increased sixfold in the first decade of the twenty-first century. In addition, the market

117 The Casablanca stock exchange was then known as the « Office de Compensation des Valeurs Mobilières ».

118 David C. L. Nellor, « Les marchés financier en Afrique: véritable outil de développement », Finance et Développement, September 2008.

capitalization of the ten largest markets increased from $222 billion to more than $700 billion over the same period, an average annual growth rate of 18%. Finally, African bonds, in local currency, have become very popular. According to data from the Emerging Markets Traders Association, from 2007 to 2009, USD 10 billion of capital was raised on eighteen stock exchanges through the listing of one hundred and seventy new companies. At the end of 2015, the capitalization of all twenty-three African stock exchanges represented one thousand four hundred billion dollars, or 60% of the continental GDP, for one thousand six hundred listed companies.

The moderate but mounting interest of investors responds to multiple stimuli: political strategies to develop popular ownership through privatization of enterprises in the late 1990s; the development of private sector enterprises seeking to finance their development; investor interest in acquiring shares in public utilities and in government bonds; and the growth of the middle class, some of whose members see stock market investment as a savings product, a long-term investment designed to provide a regular income for retirement. These are the levers of this progression.

Like in other parts of the world, the collapse of the global market in 2008 dampened the momentum of African financial markets. This led to a decline in the number of new issues, the withdrawal of investors from foreign portfolios, and the collapse of local stock market indices.

Ten years after the crisis, the question arises as to where we are now.

The need to finance companies of all sizes and start-ups is an almost universal observation. In 2006, the Stock Exchange of Mauritius (SEM) created a market dedicated specifically to small and medium-sized enterprises as well as start-ups. Four years later, fifty companies were listed on this market with a market capitalisation of nearly one thousand seven hundred and twenty-five million dollars.

The place of financial services and the need for their development in the continent's economic activity are currently subject to debate. Some of these elements are being implemented, while others are awaiting decisions.

It should be noted first and foremost that African equity markets rank second and third in international rankings. According to MSCI Inc., a New York-based financial market analyst, the stock exchanges of Egypt and South Africa are classified as emerging markets; those of Nigeria, Morocco, Tunisia, Kenya, Mauritius and, since November 2016, the Regional Stock Exchange (BRVM) as a border stock exchange.

The continent's stock exchanges represent 12 percent of the world's emerging markets, but attract less than 2 percent of portfolio investment. While it is true that repeat investors exist in Africa, investments are generally cautious and take place in the most mature and liquid markets, such as those in South Africa or Egypt. There is considerable space to be occupied. Despite their volatility, portfolio investment in emerging markets remains a potential source of financing that is still under-exploited in African markets. Their attractiveness is still limited. However, significant current and virtual progress could, in time, help to bridge this gap.

The full range of traditional financial products is available in Africa at present: equities, bonds, exchange traded funds, investment funds and other derivatives. From Mauritius to Tunis, from Casablanca to Nairobi, the managers of the continent's stock exchanges have gradually ensured this diversification of the offer. They have also added innovative financial instruments, particularly for small and medium-sized enterprises, which were previously confined to the informal sector.

The results are variable but significant, even quite impressive. At the Abidjan Regional Stock Exchange (BRVM), the composite index rose by 20%, 39%, 11% and 17% respectively for the years 2012, 2013, 2014 and 2015. Between 2012 and 2015, capitalization increased by 86% and trading volumes by 178%. In addition, the annual value of transactions rose from FCFA 146 billion to FCFA 336 billion.

This offer of financial products coincides with the growth in the volume of institutional and individual investors and the African diasporas, as shown by the results of bond issues. It also coincides with the ongoing transformation of the banking sector and its progressive offer of adapted financial services.

If the ongoing standardization process were to lead African states to sell some of their holdings in public companies, particularly oil and mining, then potential stock market giants would appear on the continent.[119] This would change the current size of several of the continent's financial centres completely. This is what the Cairo government did, with some success, to reactivate the market at the end of the 1990s, a decision that led the Egyptian Exchange in 1997 to launch its modernization program. It was estimated that the Algiers stock exchange would see its capitalisation multiplied by one hundred if the Algerian state decided to list the hydrocarbon giant Sonatrach.

---

119 These include the Gabon Oil Company, the Nigerian National Petrolium Corporation and the Algerian Sonatrach.

At the beginning of 2016, Saudi Arabia announced the listing of Saudi Aramco, the world's largest oil company with an estimated value of between two trillion and three trillion dollars. Truth in Riyadh, truth in Algiers, Libreville, Abuja, Brazaville! If this hypothesis were to be confirmed, Africa's market capitalisation would suddenly be significantly increased and several of the continent's financial centres would take off in a sensational manner.[120]

Finally, the continent's scholarships enjoy significant institutional recognition, a recognition likely to increase their activities and enhance their credibility, reliability and visibility. Thus, the inclusion of several of the continent's stock exchanges in the International Indexes noted above shows that their leaders have taken the necessary steps to meet the recognized standards in the field. Of course, as elsewhere in the world, the development of African financial markets is a long-term process that depends on several factors such as economic stability, the reliability of regulatory bodies and investment protection measures.

Finally, since we are talking about Africa and its impossible legacy of borders, it seems indispensable that a regional supply of financial services be developed, as is already the case in West Africa, to compensate for the limited size of national economies. Nicky Newton-King, the president of the Johannesburg Stock Exchange, points out that "the existence of a stock exchange is very expensive and that it is not commercially viable to have many stock exchanges on the continent".

What will it be in 2050?

By that date, how many stock exchanges and regional markets will there be on the continent? Africa's middle class of almost one billion people, including institutional investors, insurance companies, tax-advantaged savings funds, pension funds and deposit banks, all of which have substantial resources must be considered.

In the long-term, what will the current initiatives to partially integrate the markets produce?

The Southern African Development Community (SADC) stock exchanges have strengthened their integration by harmonizing their listing criteria. In East Africa, several Kenyan companies have multiple listings in Kenya, Tanzania and Uganda, as all three exchanges have established a common regulatory authority and automated transaction platform. The African Association of Stock Exchanges (AASEA), which brings together 27 stock exchanges on the continent, entered into a partnership with the African Development Bank in 2016, which

[120] Jacques Leroueil, « Chroniques », *Magazine Forbes Afrique*, March 3 2017.

led to the creation of a partnership program to support "the integration of African stock exchanges. "The Casablanca, Johannesburg and Nairobi stock exchanges were the first to join this initiative.

What will be the number of scholarships on the continent in 30 years?

How many national, sub-regional or pan-African companies listed on the stock exchange in thirty years will bring to life the scenario of African savings and capital serving mainly the development of the continent's businesses?

How many shares in the capitalization then taken by investors on the continent and what shares taken by the subsidiaries of Asian and Western multinationals?

How many stock exchanges because of the necessary agreements, associations or mergers?

An Emerging Private Sector

In this period of ever-increasing needs, the continent can count on the development of a clean private sector. Jean-Michel Sévérino and Jérémy Hajdenberg have painted a convincing picture.[121] This progress is reflected in numerous activities including the International SME Business Fair in Yaounde, the International Conference on the Emergence of Africa in Dakar, the Africa CEO Forum in Kigali, the International Trade and Industry Forum in Abidjan, the Intra-African Investment Forum in Johannesburg, the Indian Ocean Economic Forum in Mauritius, without forgetting Ethiopia which will host, in 2020, the first offshore edition of the Davos Forum, known as the World Economic Forum.[122]

The number of African companies operating across the continent is steadily increasing, affecting competition favourably and undermining, where useful, the overly close relationships between political power and domestic suppliers. In 2017, Aliko Dangote, Africa's supposedly richest businessman, launched the "AfroChampions" initiative in Lagos to mobilize the public and private sectors to support the private sector of the economy and to provide all possible support for the realization of the continental free trade area. Fifty African multinationals have signed the charter of this grouping.

---

121 Jean-Michel Severino et Jeremy Hajdenberg, « Entreprenante Afrique », Paris, Odile Jacob, 2016.

122 Idriss Linge, « L'Éthiopie sera en 2020 le premier pays, après la Suisse, à abriter le Forum économique mondial », *Ecofin Hebdo*, no.62, February 1, 2019.

Examples of African companies operating in several countries of the continent are numerous. Below are a few examples for the year 2019. Naspers, the South African multimedia group, is present throughout the continent; the Banque Marocaine du Commerce extérieur has a presence in thirty-two countries on the continent; Jumia, the online commerce platform is present in twenty-three countries; the Econet group is present in seventeen countries; PCCI, the Senegalese call company operates in fifteen African countries; the Dangote Group (cement plant), in more than fifteen countries; those of the Tunisian Group Loukil, in fifteen countries; MTN Groupo in sixteen countries; the Senegalese Group BTP, a Sahelian company, is present in ten West African countries; Shoprite Holdings has facilities in seventeen countries and Sanlam, in ten countries etc.; and the Senegalese Group BTP, a Sahelian company, is present in sixteen countries.) According to the Boston Consulting Group, this growth is due to easier access to capital and proven African expertise.

In turn, African banking groups, whose development is accelerating, increasingly belong to continental cross-border networks. In a recent study, Financial Afrik portrays twenty-five African banks with a strong regional impact, half of them operating in more than ten countries. According to economist André Ryba, "African banks that operate at the level of a single country will find it difficult to compete with regional groups. In fact, regional integration allows cross-border groups to hedge against the risks of certain investments necessary for their expansion, contributes to the increase in banking and competition and thus allows a reduction in the costs of services offered."

As previously noted, the continent is experiencing a continuous increase in demand as a result of demographic enrichment, the growth of existing cities, the development of new cities and the rise of a middle class.[123] This demand is supported by a growing number of digital companies that contribute to cross-border trade, communication consultancy firms, local and regional marketing, advertising, graphics and design companies, among others.

Finally, the continent has and will have a young, abundant and well-trained workforce, two hundred million Africans today aged between 15 and 24, a workforce that Europe and China will lack tomorrow.

As we shall see, the confidence indicators are favourable. The advocacy literature of the International Chamber of Commerce, international surveys in the field and, over the last 15 years, the continued

---

123 Deloitte, La consommation en Afrique. Le marché du XXIe siècle. 2015

arrival of major Asian business groups on the continent amply demonstrate this.

Could it be that the long-documented, desired and expected regionalisation of the continent is finally being implemented because of the progress and needs of the private sector of the economy? Could it be that the effective superimposition of the economic map on the political map will change the latter? Could the consideration of the continent as a market contribute to the consolidation of regional economic communities or could national and regional perspectives be combined and consolidated?

The Economic Development of the Continent

In the process of becoming a self-sufficient market and thus reaching the global economy, Africa is gradually appropriating the levers of its own economic development. Complex, the process will be long and marked by contrary cycles. However, it appears to be well under way and is based, in part, on advances in information technology, which can be broken down into multiple digital services. These services are increasingly being created by young African scientists or technicians and are being added to the much cited banking and/or financial services for obvious reasons.[124] Finally, incubators and Business Forums are proliferating on the continent, and it appears that the development of the entrepreneurial spirit, especially among the younger generations, is spreading at a rapid pace.

Simultaneously, financial institutions including banks, venture capital companies and insurance companies[125] are gradually shifting from former colonial powers to Africans, Moroccans, Nigerians, South Africans, Ivorians etc. It is expected that their interest in their clients, companies and markets on the continent will encourage them to reinvest their profits in Africa much more than the foreign companies that dominated the continent's market before and after independence.

As the international partners of these new African financiers diversify, due to the gradual withdrawal of certain European financial institutions, the installation on the continent of Asian financial and banking companies, including Chinese ones, and the recent interest of decision-makers in Islamic finance, African partners are expanding.

---

[124] See below in text: The deployment of the digital era.

[125] Sunu, present in fourteen countries on the continent, the Moroccan Saham Group, present in 26 countries on the continent, the Senegalese Soinan Group present in five countries.

In the insurance sector alone, the continent will have to catch up and move from 1% of GDP at present compared to 3% and 6% respectively for Latin America and Asia. The current movements point to a change in level. In 2016, "premiums grew twice as fast in Sub-Saharan Africa as the region's GDP. "The big Europeans in the field, Axa and Allianz, plus the big Moroccans, of which the powerful Saham company has taken note. They have invested hundreds of millions of dollars in sub-Saharan Africa in various forms: buyouts of companies on the continent, investments in mobile technology, a privileged way to reach new customers. [126] Finally, they have set up African management teams to give themselves a "local profile" in front of the continent's big players such as the South African companies Old Mutual and Sanlam which, following the purchase of the Moroccan company Saham Finances, have become the most important African insurance company.

Foreign financial companies no longer have continental partners but they increasingly building ties with serious international partners. Standardization is taking place gradually.

International investment movements are dependent on the slow but real change in the African market, a market of more than 1.2 billion consumers today with a growing middle class; a market of 2.4 billion in 30 years' time with a middle class that could exceed 1 billion people. "The continent has become the second most attractive destination for investment", according to the China Daily of June 30, 2015 in an article entitled: Africa Still Poised to become the Next great Investment Destination. This article was authored by Yan Li, Vice President of the African Development Bank; Makhtar Diop, Vice President of the World Bank; Li Yong, Director-General of the United Nations Industrial Development Organization; and Ato Ahmed Shide, Ethiopia's State Minister for Finance and Economic Development.

It is the prospect of a large and solvent market that has led multinationals and other Western companies into the promised lands of China, India and other Asian consumer reserves. These same prospects of the development of a vast solvent market are and will be a procession to the multinationals of the whole world, from the East but also from the West towards the promised lands of Africa. By the middle of the century, one man in four in the world will live there.

As in the case of China, colossal investments will have to be made in four strategic sectors if Africa's development is to be firmly estab-

126 Joel Té-Léssia Assoko, « Assurances Allianz passe à l'offensive pour combler son retard », *Jeune Afrique*, no 3007, August 26-September 3 2018.

lished and become an integral part of the world's industrial ecosystem by the middle of the century. Africa must have an energy lever comparable to those of other major regions of the world; it must have land, air and sea transport networks that open up the continent's regions from one another and properly link it to all regions of the world; it must modernize its agriculture and develop a substantial agri-food sector; to multiply the basis for the production of goods and services on the continent and create the millions of jobs that Africans urgently need every year; to develop the continent's cities and meet basic needs such as housing, education, health, employment, security, etc.; to develop the continent's economy and to create the conditions for the development of the continent's cities; to promote the development of the continent's economy; and to eradicate poverty.

These investments should help accelerate the establishment of non-extractive industrial facilities in the countries of the continent, since, in the words of the AfDB, "the mere exploitation of natural resources is no longer enough to meet the demand for employment and social inclusion.

The case of the Chinese Transition Company in Ethiopia is exemplary. The company has sold more than two hundred million phones on the continent over the last ten years, most of which are produced or assembled in Ethiopia at a rate of two million per month. The price is set according to the financial capacity of the customers; the technology is adjusted to take into account the environment: low lighting or even opacity of the premises for photography; difficult access to energy, hence the interest in having batteries with a longer life span.

This transition perfectly embodies China's vision of Africa's development as a growing and evolving market. This vision is based on the conviction that the continent's transformation is underway as a result of the convergence of technology, investment, urbanization and trade. This vision has been remarkably described by Howard French in his book "China's Second Continent: How a Million Migrants are building a New Empire in Africa."[127]

Like in China, zones specialized in specific productions should eventually emerge in Africa so that "MADE IN AFRICA" becomes imperative in the coming decades.

Such industrialization is slowly emerging. Cocoa beans are now processed in Cameroon and Côte d'Ivoire, whose 2015-2020 Agricultural Investment Plan also provides for the processing of coffee, cashew nuts

---

[127] Howard French, "China's Second Continent: How a million migrants are building a New Empire", in *Africa Media*, 2016.

and cotton. Textile and garment factories employ a large workforce in Kenya, Nigeria, Rwanda, Tanzania, Zambia and Ethiopia. In the latter case, the creation of two million jobs in the country's twelve industrial parks is expected by 2020.[128] «We are still an agrarian society, but this is changing,» says the National Investment Commissioner. In Guinea Conakry, Emirates Global Aluminium is embarking on the first local processing of bauxite into aluminium. Plans for the assembly of mobilized vehicles, trucks and cars, as shown earlier, are multiplying in many countries on the continent. These industrialisation movements unfolding on the continent are happening, albeit too slowly. They are insufficient to counter the high level of unemployment and to balance the balance of payments, which is suffering greatly from a high level of imports.

Moreover, important sectors of economic activity are making significant progress. One example is tourism. Indeed, "Africa is the continent that has experienced the strongest growth in tourism in the last ten years. "Between 2010 and 2016, the number of tourists has doubled, from twenty-six to fifty-six million and "it should be one hundred and thirty-four million in 2030".[129] This growth has affected several countries, including Rwanda, where tourism has become the country's main source of foreign exchange. In 2017, global increase in the number of tourists depended exclusively on that recorded in Africa, at sixty-three million.[130]

Contemplating the potential African market, the second largest in the emerging world, is a powerful stimulus for investment. Indeed, the size of the African market for consumption of goods and services could, by mid-century, be twice the size of the combined populations of Europe and North America.

Gradually, the appreciation of the current and virtual African market is shifting towards more commitments and investments, and more optimism as well. The conclusions of Havas Horizon's annual barometer for the year 2018, which analyses investors' intentions regarding Africa, are positive. "Nearly 92% of those surveyed are very optimistic about the economic outlook in Africa, and 80% of them even plan to strengthen their positions there by 2023."[131]

---

128 Bill Donahue, "To fast Fashion", *Bloomberg Businessweek*, March 5, 2018

129 Taleb Rifai, Secrétaire général de l'Organisation du tourisme, « Les forteresses touristiques ne sont pas la meilleure stratégie », *Jeune Afrique*, numéro 2947, July 2-8 2017.

130 Quartz Africa weekly brief, January 2019.

131 Marlène Panara, « L'Afrique continue à attirer les investisseurs étrangers », *Le Point Afrique*, August 3 2018.

The favourable assessment of fund managers and commercial operators is converging.

Eric Kump is the Chief Executive Officer of the Carlyle Sub-Saharan Fund. He expresses the sentiments of many of his colleagues when he confesses to being focused on the continent's "promising future" and does not hesitate to express his great enthusiasm for the opportunities that Africa offers at the moment. "Many African businesses are growing and need capital and skills...supply, demand and expectations are all good in Africa today. As an evolving ecosystem, the African market is entrepreneurial, growing and less structured than in Europe or the United States, so there are more opportunities to navigate it."[132]

Kusseni Dlamini is the President of the Massmart Group, the African branch of Wal-Mart with four hundred stores in twelve countries on the continent, forty-two of which are outside South Africa. In March 2018, at the CEO Forum in Abidjan, he announced that his group will open twenty new stores in five new countries [133] and that he is studying the market in "Francophone Africa" with a view to establishing itself there. "We are very optimistic about Africa as a whole," he added. [134]

Commenting on his team' s results for 2016, Orange CEO Stéphane Richard confesses that he has targeted the Middle East and Africa in particular, where "gross margins are slightly higher than the Group average". After recalling that its turnover had doubled there in seven years, the head of the telecommunications company then recalled that the Group has one hundred and ten million customers in Africa. He added that "the potential there is immense."

In its report for the year 2017, the African Private Equity and Venture Capital Association[135] notes that the number of its funds has continued to grow in Africa since 2010 and the volume of their investment has exceeded $20 billion. The analyst concludes on an optimistic note given the returns recorded. Between 2007 and 2017, private equity investment produced results 70% more favourable than those provided by public markets.

Announcing the creation of an Investor Confidence Indicator for Africa, the influential International Chamber of Commerce (ICC)

---

132 *Jeune Afrique*, January 14-20 2018.

133 Kenya, Ghana, Mozambique, Zambia and Swaziland.

134 Abidjan Forum CEO. Reuters, Investing news, "We are very bullish about Africa as a whole", March 22, 2018.

135 www.avca-africa.org

highlights the importance of ongoing investments in digital infrastructure and media on the continent.[136] The Chamber's staff says that "the e-commerce boom is shaking up economies around the world and will strengthen the continent's presence in international trade. »

According to the Chamber, businesses that use online sales platforms have an immensely better chance of exporting than those that do not have an Internet presence. In China, for instance, the Chamber estimates that the giant Alibaba has created 33 million jobs in its home country, with each third-party supplier using its platform creating at least three more jobs.

Investment, e-commerce and jobs have become inseparable, with the gender factor added, according to the Chamber. The chamber points out that in China, half of the registered online businesses are run by women.

Truth in China, truth in Africa!

E-Commerce in Africa

The business volume of e-commerce on a global level rose to two thousand three hundred and four billion dollars in 2017[137] or 10.2% of total retail sales compared to one thousand three hundred and thirty six billion in 2014.[138] These data illustrate both the insolent growth of online commerce, +24.8% in 2017, and the space that remains to be conquered. The eMarketer Institute predicts that its value will reach four trillion dollars in 2020, or 14.6% of total retail sales on the planet. China, with an increase of 600% between 2010-2014, leads the way in online shopping volume, followed by the United States, Great Britain, Japan, Germany, France, South Korea, Canada, Russia and Brazil.[139]

With $16 billion in online sales by 2016, India is excluded from this list, as is Africa. Yet both could dominate it by the middle of the century with respective Internet user communities of more than one billion people. Both constitute an extraordinary reserve for e-commerce and also a vast field of competition. The greats of the system, including the American Amazon, which wants to make India its second market after the United States, and the Chinese Alibaba, which

136 https://iccwbo.org/media-wall/news-speeches/5-reasons-tradematters-for-africa/

137 Its value in 2018 is estimated to be close to $3 trillion.

138 Journal du Net, « Chiffre du e-commerce dans le monde ». July 11 2018

139 Florian Marguerite, Top 10 des pays ou l'e-commerce est le plus présent. www.ecommerce-nation.fr

offers its miraculous formulas to India after having refined them in China, are the protagonists of this competition. Both of them add up local suppliers and make vast legal detours to comply with the strong demands of the Indian government which fiercely fights against "digital colonialism".

Africa is also the terrain of this rivalry in parallel with India.

It was a modest start on the mainland. However, most experts predict a rapid consolidation of the conditions favourable to its expansion: continued growth of smartphone users, which will reach 660 million by 2020 and an increase of half a billion Africans who have access to the Internet; access to and strong use of mobile payment formulas that make up for the lack of banking services[140]; development of 3G and 4G; slow upgrading of logistical infrastructures that open up communities and ensure greater autonomy for individuals. The results are spectacular. The Kenya Commercial Bank, for example, has seen its clients jump from two million to seventeen million in less than ten years.

This trade has generated a revenue of fifty billion dollars in 2016, a revenue that grows by 8.5% per year and could reach one hundred and sixteen billion in 2025, according to the report "Lion go digital: The Internet's transformative potential in Africa", by the McKinsey Co. firm. The research firm Disrupt Africa, for its part, has identified two hundred sixty-four companies that supply goods or services via e-commerce in twenty-three African markets, with food, capital goods, clothing, transport and travel being principal industries.

Created in 2013, the company JUMIA is the leading distributor on the continent. Headquartered in Dubai, the company has logistics chains, warehouses and distribution systems in fourteen countries on the continent and benefits from the contribution of four thousand employees. As of 2016, the company had over half a billion visitors, offered five million products, completed more than one million transactions and launched a mobile payment system, Jumia Pay, based on the Amazon Pay, AliPay or MercadoPago models. More than 70% of Jumia's customers access its platform via mobile devices. In 2017, Jumia's sales experienced spectacular growth of 70%.

The South African companies Stainhoff and Shoplist, the Congolese Konga.ca, the Ghanaian Kasoa, the Nigerian Kaymu and MallforAfrica.com plus a large number of companies whose operations are limited to the national territory follow. The combined sales of this constellation of e-commerce companies on the continent would have

140 Kenya's leading bank, Kenya Commercial Bank, conducts 90% of its transactions over the Internet.

reached $50 billion in 2017, not counting the high volume of online sales of new and used vehicles.[141] According to the Ecofin agency, African e-commerce is expected to double every five years to reach three hundred and fifty billion dollars by 2035.

Recently, major players in the field are moving closer to the continent. eBay has partnered with the Nigerian MallforAfrica.com; Amazon.fr has recently sought to extend its operations from France to Africa, but without success.

Chinese e-commerce companies, including Kikuu and Kilimall, are planning their activities in this vast upcoming continental market. They already have the indispensable tool for transactions of all kinds, with more than 700 million mobile devices today and more than 1 billion in 2050.

The market is appropriate for Chinese giants in the field, who have mastered the techniques that work in emerging markets. At the end of 2017, Alipay counted five hundred and twenty million users and daily transactions of between twenty and twenty-five billion, 90% of which were carried out using smartphones.[142] A competitor, Tencent (WeChat Pay), has a comparable offer and business volume.

In 2016, the digital economy accounted for 30% of China's GDP, and online payments in the same year totaled five thousand five hundred billion dollars, fifty times more than the one hundred and twelve billion spent in the United States.[143] Analysts of this new economy argue that the shift away from cash payments reduces costs, reduces dubious manipulation and corruption, drives people out of the informal economy and expands the tax base.

In the battle for African customers and the deployment of e-commerce on the continent, China enjoys definite advantages, as the Chinese and African markets, though different, offer notable similarities. A clientele that is partly rural and unbanked, and which, twenty years ago, in very large numbers, did not have identity cards or biometric identification forms in China. These situations prevail today in Africa. A Chinese clientele that has entered digital civilization via mobile phones, as in Africa; a young clientele, 70% of whom are under thirty years old, as in Africa; a clientele that is looking for products and accessories adapted to its style, needs and resources. The contrast between eBay's streamlined interface to suit the tastes of Westerners and Alib-

141 https://store.frost.com/

142 Exclusive Access, *The Economist*, May, 5th, 2018.

143 « Le grand bond des « licornes » chinoises », *Le Monde*, September 19, 2017.

aba's, "a jumbled site, teeming with information and advertising, like a big bazaar", was even mentioned.[144]

Created by the World Bank in 2012, the Fintex Index shows the decisive impact of technologies on people's financial inclusion. In 2012, 2.5 billion people in the world were unbanked, 1.7 billion five years later.

Alibaba's boss Jack Ma visited Kenya and Rwanda in the summer of 2017. It seems that the experience of the large Chinese group in China and emerging countries is transferable to the African market. This is undoubtedly what Alibaba's boss had in mind when he inaugurated a first regional sales platform in Kigali in 2017. This is the viewpoint of executives of several pioneering African companies in the field, including Jumia, which are benefiting from the help of the Chinese giant. The latter is aiming for a wider implantation on the continent. Its leaders are already talking about "helping African producers to promote what they have to offer on the global digital market. Much more than the admonitions of international organizations, these developments are and will be affecting African politics, as Nangala Nyahola has shown in his important book: How the Internet is transforming Politics in Kenya.[145]

Still, the United States and China are the only world powers that have managed to master the digital processes necessary for e-commerce in their entirety. This means that this maze of technology, which sustains the global industry, is in their hands. According to Rich Lesser's assessment as highly respected CEO of the Boston Consulting Group (BCG), China "is already conducting business with five of the world's top ten digital players and its economy is the most digitalized in the world. In this country, living online is synonymous with living."[146]

The Russian Federation, for its part, has its own system whose influence extends only as far as the countries of Central and Eastern Europe, where there are large Russian-speaking minorities. Europe and India, by contrast, have failed to develop the technological architecture required to offer the world the full range of services of the digital age.

The countries and regions of the African continent mirror the experience of virtually every country in the world. They have not

---

144 *Le Monde*, idem.

145 Nanjala Nyahola, "How the Internet Era is transforming Politics in Kenya. Nairobi", Zed Books, 2018.

146 Le Grand témoin: Rich Lesser, PDG du Boston consulting Group, *Le Figaro* December 3, 2017.

endowed themselves with the technological maze that supports all the operations of the digital civilization. Neither dramatic delays nor spectacular advances have been made in connecting to the global systems that provide the basic services carried by digital power. But the continent is and will be strained between the American system and the Chinese system. The choices being made in this area will have a major impact on global economic and digital development, as the continent has, by the middle of the century, taken steps to add one billion or so e-consumers (prosumers) to the clienteles already acquired by the Chinese or American giants in the field.[147]

In addition, the continent has and will have need of its own technological relays, particularly satellite technology, to meet its many commercial, meteorological, environmental, agricultural, maritime, security, resource management, research, education and health needs.

For a quarter of a century, satellites have been providing the continent with services for financial exchanges such as the Sat3Play platform, for the leasing of bands making continental connectivity possible. This makes possible the deployment of major projects such as the Pan-African Network for Tele-Health and Tele-Education promoted by the African Union and the Indian government, such as the NEPAD project to install Internet connectivity in more than six hundred thousand schools.[148]

The current and virtual African market is and will be the battlefield of the two digital powers that will want to appropriate it, as are the European and Indian markets at present. Thus the Alibaba Group is investing massively to create an ecosystem of B2B services in Europe, including e-commerce, entertainment, payment, cloud computing, artificial intelligence, physical commerce, etc. This future availability of global systems will be an opportunity for African producers to take their offer to the world.

This expansion is in line with President Xi's global plan, the famous "Made in China 2025", which aims to be at the forefront in an impressive range of fields: robotics, semiconductors, electric vehicles, artificial intelligence, etc.[149] The recent FOCAC announcement that China and the African Union are stepping up work to deploy an integrated communications infrastructure network in Africa illustrates

---

147 "Tech firms in emerging markets. Clash of the Titan", *The Economist*, July 7, 2018.

148 CGECI, Télécommunication: Un satellite propre à l'Afrique en orbite. April 14, 2018.

149 "China's Pole-to-Pole Ambitions", *Bloomberg Newsweek*, September 3, 2018.

this policy. In addition, it supports investments by Chinese companies to increase connectivity on the continent.

The continent and its people also benefit and will benefit from the ripple effects of scientific and technological innovations, such as Internet access, the use of satellites, and the use of artificial intelligence. Innovation is transforming the way goods and services are produced and will continue to do so on the continent, as it has in other parts of the world. As Pony Ma Huateng, the president of Tencent, suggests, it will be able to create both financial wealth and levers for the less well-off communities.[150]

For the foreseeable future, African societies will benefit from the analysis of data that will study behaviours, identify expectations and propose opportunities for Africans. The inhabitants of these urban societies, the majority of whom are young and proud users of new technologies, will be involved in the process of collecting, analyzing and interpreting data detailing whole sections of their lives. Rwanda, Egypt, Nigeria, Morocco, Tunisia, Senegal, Ghana, Côte d'Ivoire, Kenya, South Africa and Tunisia would be in a position to launch analyses of the metadata available to them.

It remains for these countries to acquire, individually or in partnership, computing power in national or regional data centres on the continent. The aim is to avoid processing the data outside the continent and avoid the loss of the considerable benefits that could ensue. Built by algorithms, the syntheses of these data must be thought out and structured according to African realities, needs and interests. They must not be transformed into foreign data and, like looted works of art and natural resources, must eventually be classified as imported goods. This has gone on long enough in the case of Africa.

Like the rest of the world, the societies and people of the continent are likely to benefit greatly from these potentials as they are constructed, mastered, interpreted and used by them. It is important that the continent's governments, researchers and entrepreneurs seize these technologies, master them and use them for the benefit of Africans.

Together with Asian and Western partners, these technology transfers must be at the top of all the lists subject to joint analysis. They must also include the fundamentals of cultural digital production and access to the most advanced distribution systems. Netflix, in its own inadequate but real way, has paved the way by creating a kind of lottery for the continent's filmmakers and directors. The latter will be

150 Pony Ma Huateng, "Doing good by doing tech", *The Economist*, The World in 2019.

able to propose their film or TV series projects for financing to the Californian company. In return, it will offer them in continuous flow on its networks around the world.

Investment: The Top Priority

Some major investments underway on the continent include the renovated old ports of Lomé, Dakar, Abidjan, Acra and Coega are located, in addition to new ports such as Bagamoyo in Tanzania, Lamu in Kenya and Nqura in South Africa, from Kribi south of Douala, that of Tangier on the Strait of Gibraltar, which links the continent to Europe, that of Doraleh in Djibouti, which links the continent to Asia, the ports under construction of Lekki and Badagry in Nigeria, which will be the largest deep-water port on the continent, not forgetting the ports announced in the Suez Canal economic zone. By granting these colossal investments, the major world logistics operators are signalling their confidence in the future of the continent. In particular, they take note of the current and virtual growth in demand for goods from Africa, and also of the growth in African demand, with two hundred and sixty five million tonnes transported in 2009 and two billion tonnes in 2040.

Our astronauts would see vast fields of mirrors waiting for daybreak to capture the sun's energy, bunches of wind turbines from Ashegoda in Ethiopia, those of the Lake Tukana wind farm in Kenya, those of the huge Tarfaya wind farm in the Moroccan Sahara, wind farms in South Africa and, close to the coast, within sight, in Côte d'Ivoire, bunches of wind turbines between Grand-Bassam and Abidjan.

They would see beams of light coming from new city neighbourhoods or new cities under construction.

They would also see trails of light between Djibouti and Adis Ababa and, even further north towards Egypt, Tangier and Casablanca, southern and northern Nigeria, Abuja-Abidjan and Dakar, Abidjan, Ouagadougou and Niamey, which are, among others, the continent's new rail and land routes; in addition to the light nets that follow the route of the future gas pipeline from Nigeria to Spain via Morocco.

They would also see points of light indicating new university laboratories, factories under construction, nearly completed hydroelectric power plants, brand new airports, tourist areas where they were not expected, in Madagascar.

They would see the new African museums of this century such as the superb Zeitz Mocaa in Cape Town, the largest museum of contemporary art in the world; the Zulu museum in Durham by the famous Ghanaian architect, David Adjaye; the beautiful building of the Zinsou Foundation in Cotonou; the Museum of Black Civilizations in Dakar, the Maacal museum in Marrakech, the Amazigh heritage museum, the superb cultural space created by the painter Aboudia in Bingerville, on the outskirts of Abidjan. They would also see agricultural cooperatives that are gables on the street.

From their own skies, our astronauts would also see too much distance between these luminous fragments, vast spaces without brightness waiting for their share of light. It is to fill these "vast inhabited or uninhabited spaces" that Africa needs investment, a colossal, urgent and sustainable need.

The battle for investment in Africa must be fought for what it is: priority of priorities over all other approaches.

The example of China is convincing and indisputable. It is the trillions of dollars and more invested in China year after year since the 1990s that has propelled it to the top of the global economy. Gradually Africa is gaining on this ground thanks to a better mobilization of its own resources and its growing attractiveness to foreign investors, its current and future market, this lever of paramount importance. In fact, since the 1990s, as we have already noted, new investors have committed themselves to the continent. One spontaneously thinks of China, but also of India, Russia, Indonesia, Vietnam, Turkey, the United Arab Emirates, etc.

Africa urgently and imperatively needs investment because of its demographic and urban enrichment, which are not possible variables, but rather ongoing developments. It needs much more than public development aid, a substantial part of which remains in the so-called donor countries, public development aid that keeps the recipients dependent and precarious, atrophies their own capacities to propose, innovate and implement and creates nothing sustainable. Published in 2007, the striking theses of the Zambian economist, Dambisa Moyo, are still relevant today.[151]

Admittedly, humanitarian support must be available on the ground, in Africa and elsewhere in the world, in the event of natural disasters or other calamities. Co-managed, government-to-government service contracts, for significant periods and in areas agreed by Africans are also acceptable, contracts modelled on investment with imperatives of results.

---

151 Dambisa Moyo, « L'aide fatale: les ravages d'une aide inutile et de nouvelles solutions pour l'Afrique », Paris, JC Lattès, 2009.

All these annual or even five-year plans, often involving derisory sums of money, favour the negotiating industry and the political clientele of the foreign donor more than the citizens of the so-called recipient country. African governments must extricate themselves from this continuous parade of donors who give nothing. It is in their interest to focus on partners that provide investments for responsible durations in intrinsic support of national priorities.

A wide range of stakeholders are or should be involved in enriching investment in Africa: local and national governments, African and foreign banks, national, regional, continental and international financial institutions, African stock exchanges, sovereign wealth funds of more than 20 African states, African and international investment funds, African and foreign companies.[152]

There are multiple flows of capital globally and in Africa that constitute the indispensable levers for the creation of economic, social and cultural wealth. In addition to the development of their own sectors which welcome investment, States will quickly find their interest in it, the economic activity thus enriched contributing to the increase of their own income as never before in cooperation programmes and contributing by the same token to the implementation of national programmes.

It should be noted that a large number of African states have undertaken and succeeded in profound macroeconomic reforms, as documented by think tanks and analysis groups. One thinks in particular of the work of the Cercle de Réflexion et d'Échanges des dirigeants des administrations fiscales (CREDAF) and the studies of specialists in the field, those of Serge Patrice Ekombo[153] and Alain Symphorien Ndjana.[154]

In 2015, five African states were among the top ten in the world in terms of improving their management. Moreover, the continent accounted for one-third of the major regulatory reforms registered in the same year.[155]

Fluctuating in line with Africa's strong growth in the first decade of the century[156], slowing after the 2008-2009 crisis but becoming

152 Sovereign Wealth Fund Institute – http://www.swfinstitute.org

153 Serge Patrice Ekombo, « Stratégies de consentement à l'impôt dans les pays les moins avancés ». *Le jour*, no 2627, February 16 2018.

154 Alain Symphorien Ndjana, « Sauvons l'impôt pour préserver l'État », Paris, Le Pathéon, 2018.

155 2015, Doing Business rankings for 2013-2014.

156 5.3% compared to the world average of 4%.

more robust than in Europe or the United States[157] afterwards, having risen again but unevenly, investment on the continent flows from multiple sources.

Investment flows from Asia occupy a special place both because of their nature, in part as patient capital so important for infrastructure and industrialisation, and because of their diversity: banks, private and public companies and specialized investment funds. Among many others, we recall the following funds.

China has been the main contributor of capital to the continent since 2017 and is home to the China-Africa Development Fund to support investments by Chinese companies on the continent.[158] It also houses the China-Africa Industrial Capacity Cooperation Fund for investment in infrastructure; the China Fund for Growth in Africa; and a whole range of programmes stemming from the Forum on China-Africa Cooperation (FOCAC).

Some Singaporean companies, including the Olam Group, which has a presence in more than 20 African countries, have successfully established real operations in Africa. "Olam Gabon," writes Julien Wagner in Jeune Afrique, "has grown so rapidly that it has become the country's largest private company and the state's leading partner in activities as diverse as agriculture, industry and transport."[159]

The Japanese aim is to match China's progress and house the following funds: The Global Innovative Technology Fund (GHIT), which focuses on health, and a whole range of programs arising from the Tokyo International Conference on African Development (TICAD). These programs focus, among other things, on human resource development and infrastructure.

India currently holds third place in terms of growth, more than 7.5% annually. It houses the India Trust Fund, the India-Africa Development Fund and the India-Africa Health Fund. In addition, significant lines of credit have been provided to support Indian companies wishing to invest in the continent.

Korea is increasing its presence on the continent, notably by opening offices of the Korean Investment Agency in seven countries on the continent in 2019-2020. It is also financing 61 major projects, including the construction of an agro-industrial complex in Ethiopia,

---

157 Plus 2% in Africa, minus 4%, 2.8% and 1.5% respectively in the United States, Europe and Latin America.

158 Youmani Jérome Lankoandé, « Économie politique des investissements directs de la Chine en Afrique », Bruxelles, Éditions universitaires européennes, 2009.

159 *Jeune Afrique*, no 3004, August 5-11, 2018.

the establishment of an electricity grid in Tanzania, the financing of power plants in Egypt and Botswana and, with the AfDB, a technology transfer operation on UAVs for data collection and analysis for agricultural development. This cooperation includes the creation of a Korean-African UAV Research and Training Centre.

Flows from Europe remain significant: private equity funds such as those of the French groups Meridian Infrastructure Africa Fund (MIAF) and Vivo Energy; mixed funds such as those resulting from the agreement that now links the French government's Official Development Assistance own resources and the vast reserves of the French *Caisse de dépôt et consignation*. For its part, Germany, within the G7 framework, has proposed a Marshall Plan for Africa.[160] Regrettably, European countries are drawn, in succession, towards forms of nativism. Even Germany is being courted by this retrogression.[161]

An important contribution comes from America, which houses numerous action funds, some of which are highly influential. These include the One Thousand & One Voices Investment Fund, the Carlyle Group Fund, and the CDC Group which, through its CDC Fund Africa, manages fifty-eight specialized funds invested in thirty-eight countries on the continent.[162] In addition, there are the South American Funds, including the important Brazilian Fund of the BTG Pactual Bank.

The most recent American literature on investment in Sub-Saharan Africa is positive. According to several companies in the field, the situation has changed significantly as a result of the improved political environment and economic development.[163]

Investment streams from the continent are increasingly significant: banks, African companies targeting the continental or even global market; African workers' pension funds, including, for example, the Social Security Fund; African Rainbow Capital Investment (South Africa); and the Citadel Capital Fund (Egypt).

Africans are also involved in a wide range of joint initiatives such as the Investment Funds set up by the Islamic Development Corporation and the African Jaiz Banks, the Wema Bank; the South-South

160 Ministère fédéral de la coopération économique et du développement, « L'Afrique et l'Europe: un nouveau partenariat pour le développement, la paix et l'avenir », Berlin, 2017.

161 Alan Crawford, "As Merkel's Power Ebbs, Europe's Peril Grows", *Bloomberg Businessweek*, July 2, 2018.

162 www.cdcgroup.com

163 www.afigfounds.com

Cooperation Fund set up by the People's Bank of China and the African Development Bank; and the India-Africa Development Fund, among several others.

Finally, as mentioned earlier, the various operations underway to bring together or even merge certain African stock exchanges have now been formalized. Concluded in 2016, the agreement between the Association of African Stock Exchanges and the African Development Bank should normally accelerate the integration of the continent's stock exchanges by region, initially. In early 2019, the president of the Association announced the allocation of a Korean fund dedicated to the interconnection of the continent's stock exchanges. These various movements have and will have the effect of facilitating the raising of African equity capital and making it available for investment.

This progressive appropriation of the levers of their development by Africans is also manifested in the gradual rise of professional services and consultancy firms that they are developing. Thus, the virtual monopoly exercised by foreign offices on the analysis and definition of the needs of the African private or public sectors is coming to a close. With regard to engineering offices, they include the Guinean company l'Africaine d'Études et d'ingénierie Financière, the Ivorian companies Bani, Bergec, and CECAF International, the Togolese company Deco-IC, the Senegalese companies Cabinet Merlin, ETECS, Gaudillat, the Tunisian company BETA, the Moroccan companies Ben Bassou, Maprelec, Lénos Engineering among many others. As far as architects are concerned, an African weekly magazine has drawn up an impressive list: from the Ivorian firm Guillaume Kuff to the South African Makeba Deseign, from the Senegalese Lamtono to the Malian So-Da Architecte without forgetting the Cameroonian Financia Capital and the Beninese Agence Athus. In terms of consulting firms, the following are particularly worth mentioning: Actu Conseil from Côte d'Ivoire; Valyans Consulting and Capital Consulting Group from Morocco; Performances Management Consulting Group and ACT Afrique Group from Senegal.

The consultancy services provided by these new entities are expected to have a significant impact on the destination of investments and their correlation with the needs of the continent. Such should be the consequences of an expertise better adjusted to the realities and priorities of African societies, of a broader and finer knowledge of the needs of the continent and its operators.

This development has led to the establishment of branches or subsidiaries of the large international consulting groups which, until then, defined the needs of the continent from London, Paris, New York or Brussels. All the major consulting firms now have facilities on the continent: McKinsey &Co but also, Okan, strategy and financial consulting, the Euro Group consulting, the Boston consulting Group, Frost & Sullivan, Cap Gemini Consulting, Deloitte, KPMG and Emerson, among many others.

The effects of these various movements are to ensure the development of African expertise, create professional networks, associate designers and operators, in addition to maintaining capital in Africa, perhaps also paying special attention to local materials, social traditions and heritage resources of African societies. This also manifests itself at the political level. President Kagame, Chairman of the African Union, stated, not without pride: "Never have the endogenous funds devoted to the prevention and intervention capacities of our peacekeeping forces been at such a high level as they are today". That same year, Akinwumi Adesina, the President of the African Development Bank, published his bank's Report, a first, in Swahili, Haussa, Arabic, plus the predictable Western languages.

It is also important to note that the continent now has access to patient development capital for the first time in its history for long-term investment, including in particular the upgrading or construction of public facilities; the development of land, rail, sea or air transport infrastructure; the construction of hydroelectric power stations, and so on. China has mapped out this path. A large number of our African interlocutors have told us, in various forms, that "China is a true partner, the only one today that works on long-term cooperation," in the words of the President of Djibouti, Ismail Omar Guelleh.[164]

Perspectives on Africa

According to The Economist, investment funds dedicated to sub-Saharan Africa have doubled between 2008-2014: national[165], regional[166] or continental.[167] They are proprietary, mixed, composed of African

---

164 Ismael Omar Guelleh, « Djibouti est libre de ses choix », *Afrique Magazine*, February 2018.

165 The example of Senegal: Terenga Capital; Fonds souverain d'investissement stratégique; l'Africaine d'investissements participatifs and its digital platform; Fonds d'appui à l'investissement des Sénégalais de l'extérieur among many others. Funds with continental vocation and activities: AFIG, Mauritius Fund; South African Fund...

166 Funds with regional vocation and activities: AFIG, Mauritius Fund; South African Fund...

167 Funds with continental vocation: Enko Africa Private Equity Fund (South Africa); Madison Financial Services PLC (Zambia). Funds with partners:

investors and institutional, governmental or private partners.[168] These funds have been created for the known universal reason: the search for an optimal return on investment, the variants of calculation determining the nature of the investments.

Some so-called "patient" investments are of longer duration and the expected return is, consequently, deferred according to agreed schedules. Other reasons are specific to Africa: "IMF forecasts of per capita growth, which, compared to those of other developing countries, are higher in countries on the continent".[169]

Until recently, it had become essential to overcome the insensitivity of banks, particularly European banks established on the continent, regarding access to banking and financial services adjusted to the realities and capacities of African corporate or individual clients, when it came to supporting the development of the African production sector. We will never know the extent of the economic and social costs that such a policy has entailed. One only has to imagine, over a period of half a century, the massive withdrawal of financial and banking services from any so-called developed country to measure the impact.

This situation has evolved recently as a consequence, as we have established earlier, of the gradual withdrawal of European financial and banking institutions, the development of African banks and banking groups "which are now at the forefront of the banking sector. "These include Ecobank, created in 1985 and present in thirty-four countries; the Bank of Africa Group, created in 1982 and present in twenty countries; the expansion on the continent of Nigerian banks (GT Bank, UBA, Zenith Bank, Access Bank); the development of regional banks (BGFI Bank, Oragroup, Afriland first Bank, Equity Bank, Kenya Commercial Bank, BankABC). Finally, the arrival on the continent of Asian and especially Chinese financial and banking institutions adds substantially to the transformation of the continent's financial system.

These favourable developments must be acknowledged and supported. Admittedly, the successive cycles of the world economy vary the weight of the financial spin-offs resulting from the exploitation of the vast natural resources with which the continent is so richly endowed. This weight of financial and economic benefits from the exploitation of

---

African Development Bank (ADB) and Banque populaire as well as ADB and India.

168 International Finance Corporation, Transformer le développement de l'Afrique. Washington, 2016.

169

natural resources is likely to diminish in the foreseeable future. Such will be the combined effects of increased investment in infrastructure, the development of land, sea and air transport, urban development including the housing sector, the development of the service economy and the continued growth of business and household consumption. Already, Chinese investments in Africa are concentrated, up to 50%, in financial services, construction, public works and manufacturing investment development.

There is also a need to rely on indigenous investment, including the various forms of African savings, including sovereign wealth funds from African countries. These savings are expected to grow steadily and the resulting capital is expected to be invested, at least in part, in the development of African economies.

The works, plans, specifications, contracts, etc. required by the announced growth of the continent's cities, plus 100% by 2040, come to mind.

Another consideration includes works, plans, specifications and contracts required to upgrade existing airports and build new ones in response to the strong increase in air traffic announced, "a real Eldorado", i.e. 5.7% annual growth for the next two decades.

Moreover, various new equipment, warehouses and maintenance services are being envisaged, as required for the growth of the fleet of aircraft serving the continent at an estimated cost of one hundred and sixty billion dollars.

Finally, the development of the service economy comes to mind. In the insurance sector alone, the continent is lagging far behind, which should normally be made up. It now represents 1% of GDP compared to 3% and 6% respectively for Latin America and Asia. Professionals in the field are working on it as shown by the work of the Inter-African Conference on Insurance Markets and the requirements of the Organization for the Harmonization of Business Law in Africa.

The social needs of Africans, including security, housing, public health and sanitation services and educational services for the hundreds of millions of children who will be joining the continent's school systems by 2050, are also being addressed.

The gradual establishment of a financial, economic and commercial ecosystem that places African operators in a comparable or even favourable position vis-à-vis foreign operators constitutes a major standardization. In a sense, the continent is taking its share of the DNA of the economy as practiced by all countries and economic groupings in the world.

Supply management, proposal of reciprocity, preferential policy for African operators, rejection of dumping which has so dramatically slowed down, even suffocated African economies: the States of the continent must negotiate closely. They now have the means to do so. At this stage and for a reasonably long time, they must protect the various production sectors that are gradually developing on the continent. The American president named, in simple terms, the actual or sought-after practice of all states. The "Africa First" mindset has a lot of little cousins around the world that don't speak their names! There are major exceptions to this position, including nuclear arms control, the climate situation and the control of disruptive technologies such as artificial intelligence and biological engineering.

By the same token, the demographic dividend should gradually reinforce a more central positioning of the continent in world affairs.

Indeed, it is likely that the reduction in the European Union's place on the international stage will become more pronounced in the coming decades, "with demographic, economic and strategic indicators all pointing to this gradual decline".

How far will the deconstruction of the European Union go? This is a question that is worth raising. As is the case of rethinking the structure of the African Union, which at mid-century represented a quarter of humanity. Theoretically and virtually, it was one of the three major poles of world affairs in the twenty-first century. Under the authority of the President of Rwanda, in 2018, the continental organisation adopted a vast reform programme aimed in particular at financial autonomy. It is to be hoped that this programme will be implemented within the planned time frame. It is essential to ensure the international political repositioning of the continent.

A Diaspora to Gather and Mobilize

China's transition from the largest and poorest country in the world[170], with a per capita income of eighty-nine dollars in 1960, to the status of the world's second economic power, with a per capita income of eight thousand dollars in 2016, has been made possible in particular by the massive and continuous investment in China by the rich Chinese diaspora..[171]

170 Jérôme Élie, Marylène Lieber and Christine Lutringer, « Migration et développement: les politiques de la Chine et de l'Inde à l'égard de leurs communauté d'outre-mer », International Development Policy, 2011.

171 Gilles Tanguay, « La diaspora chinoise, une puissance financière », *L'Expansion*, 01-11-2003.

At the end of the previous century, the latter controlled 60% of the GDP of Indonesia, Thailand and Malaysia and more than two-thirds of the turnover of the two hundred and fifty largest companies in the Philippines. Already considerable, this positioning is enriched by four other sources that bring a high level of investment to mainland China, Taiwan, Hong Kong, Macao and Singapore. Western and Asian private companies have joined this powerful cohort and, in a quarter of a century, these continuous flows of capital have lastingly changed the economic map of the world to China's advantage.[172] The OECD has called these flows "the largest transfer of wealth in human history."

Such movements did not occur in the case of India and Africa. Neither had relays comparable to China's in the world that could create far-reaching capital and technology flows.

Admittedly, the Indian diaspora has since been mobilized by New Delhi with interesting results, but these are in no way comparable to the massive results achieved by the Chinese diaspora.[173]

Fragmented like the continent, the African diaspora, which is its "deterritorialized" fragment, counts 140 million individuals. Regarded as a "symbolic African entity", the African Union has qualified it as the 55th African State, and it contributes to the continent's economy to the tune of fifty-five billion dollars annually.[174] However, to date, its full potential has not been exploited except by a few countries including Rwanda, Ethiopia, Nigeria, Morocco, Mali, Senegal and a few others. With commitment, this potential can make a difference. One example is the strong financial contribution of the Rwandan diaspora to the Crystal Ventures Investment Fund. This fund has significant capital, with strong holdings in a large number of companies in the country. It is managed by the Singaporean Kok Foong Lee.

According to Gabriel Fal, in order to get the most out of the African Diaspora, it would be necessary to establish a mapping of the existing diasporas within Africa and where there are no national banking networks in the countries of residence, use the networks of churches,

---

172 Qixu Chen, « Répartition géographique des investissements directs étrangers en Chine, Économies et Finances », Université d'Auvergne, Clermont-Ferrand, 2004.

173 Jean-Louis Roy, « Quel avenir pour la langue française »? Montréal, Hurtubise HMH, 2008.

174 Gabriel Fal, « Diasporas, les oubliés des émissions obligataires », *Jeune Afrique*, no 2984, March 18-24, 2018.

professional associations, community radio and the Internet. A better understanding of the African diasporas may reveal that they are available not only for remittances but also for commercial and social investment in the countries of origin, for knowledge and technology transfers, and for credit facilities needed especially by the continent's young entrepreneurs.

Chapter Three

Areas for Growth Potential

The category is so broad that it could have contained chapters on education, the environment, agriculture and agri-food, and so many other topics. We had to choose. The themes finally chosen will determine the ability of Africans to incorporate changes in the world and create wealth: from the energies of the future to air, land and sea mobility, not forgetting space.

The energies of the future

The continent and its people will also benefit in the coming years from a major energy revolution. The extreme lack of communication that has so limited Africa's and Africans' development over the past half century is at least partly being met by mobile phones, with 327 million subscribers in 2010, 660 million in 2018 and 725 million in 2020. The same momentum should gradually make up for the extreme energy shortage in this region of the world, a major energy producer, a shortage that has limited the development of Africa and Africans over the last half-century.

This development is due in particular to Chinese investments on the continent in renewable energies, mainly devoted to hydroelectricity, investments amounting to nearly ninety billion dollars since 2010. According to the International Energy Agency's report for 2016, 46% of new energy capacity in sub-Saharan Africa is the result of investments and work by Chinese companies. "One out of every two new megawatts is Chinese, it says. »

For its part, the Solar Alliance has set itself the goal of mobilizing $1 trillion for solar energy development by 2030.[175] In concrete terms, major solar installations are multiplying on a continent that has an unparalleled amount of sunshine, three thousand hours a year or at least six hours a day. These installations can be found in all major regions of the continent: Sinthiou Mékhé and Senergy2 in Senegal; Jasper-Kalkbult in South Africa; Zagtouli in Burkina Faso; Agalrga in Mauritius; Grand Banjul in Zambia; Kaduna in Nigeria; Rwamagana in Rwanda; Desertec and Noorl-Ouarzazate in Morocco, the latter being the largest solar power plant in the world. [176] It has the largest installed capacity with over two hundred megawatts.

Thanks to the multiplication of solar panel construction companies in Africa and also to lower prices made possible by Chinese construction and consumption, tens of millions of solar panels are produced annually (500 million worldwide for the year 2017) that bring and will bring to Africans energy and all that it provides, security, investment, employment, quality of life etc..

Numerous initiatives support this need: to finally give the half a billion Africans who are deprived of it access to energy at affordable costs. Akon Lighting Africa is one of the best known of these initiatives.[177] It is named after a world star of hip hop, the American-Senegalese singer and producer Akon, whose real name is Alioune Badara Thiam. Launched in 2014, it is being rolled out in thousands of educational institutions in four hundred localities in fifteen countries. It reaches hundreds of thousands of people who benefit from the street lamps, school or household kits, micro-networks, lamps etc. Finally, the operation has produced five thousand five hundred direct jobs.

Africa will have other options in the coming years. The option offered by the California-based company Acquantis is now being tested in the Gulf Stream, the north coast of Brazil and the coast of South Africa.[178] The idea is to dive into the sea, slightly transforming the famous propellers that collect wind energy to capture the energy

---

175 Michael Reza Pacha, « Un avenir brillant pour le solaire africain ». *Tribune Afrique*, May 20, 2018.

176 This solar power plant, which will have cost $3 billion, will provide energy to more than one million Moroccans in 2018.

177 www.akonlightingafrica.com

178 Ellem Huet, "What works for Wind power could also work under the sea", *Bloomberg Businessweek*, June 2016.

from the waves, tides and ocean currents. The system has the advantage of continuous production, day and night. Experiments on the maintenance and repair of the equipment, elevating the turbines to the heart of the turbines or bringing them to the surface for maintenance and repair, do not yet allow a choice to be made, let alone a price per kilometre of energy produced, which should not exceed that of solar energy.

Finally, since a choice has to be made, the new generations of batteries offer, according to Natacha Gorwitz, unprecedented storage possibilities for domestic, industrial or transport use. Supported by the World Bank and the African Development Bank, South Africa's Eskom is carrying out an "ambitious storage plan" that could eventually make a vital contribution to meeting the continent's energy needs.[179]

These advances should make a major contribution to the development of the continent and the consolidation of the areas that are essential to it. These include the essential air, land and sea transport sectors.

Air mobility

In the aeronautics sector, the International Air Transport Association (IATA) predicts that world air traffic will double by 2036 and a total of seven billion, eight hundred million passengers.[180] By that date, China will be the world's largest air market with one billion five hundred million passengers, followed by the United States with one billion one hundred million, India with four hundred and seventy-eight million and Africa with two hundred and fifty million compared to one hundred and twenty million in 2017.

The annual growth rate of world air traffic for the next fifteen years is expected to be 3.6%. The highest average growth rate in the world will be 5.9% in Africa. The continent will be followed by the Middle East, Asia-Pacific, Europe and North America with growth rates of 5%, 4.6% and 2.3% respectively. Tony Tyler, Director General of IATA confirms: "The highest aviation potential is on the African continent.

This progress will be greatly facilitated by important initiatives currently underway. These include investments to upgrade existing airports or to create new ones, the creation of the Single Air Transport Market program launched in January 2017 by the African Union[181]

179 Natacha Gorwitz, « Énergie – Volts en stock », *Jeune Afrique*, no. 3024.

180 « IATA: Un trafic aérien mondial doublé d'ici 2030! » *Actualité*, Perspective, October 27, 2017.

181 Kennedy Kimanthi, « Un ciel africain pour tous », *The East African*, Nairobi, February 6, 2018.

and the sector support program developed jointly by the AfDB and IATA.

This support necessarily involves supporting regional air transport, which is expected to make significant progress over the next two decades. The sector is buoyant and can be broken down into multiple formulas: partnerships between companies such as those linking Air Côte d'Ivoire, Air France and Ethiopia or Rwandair and the Beninese government, among many others.

Against this backdrop, the continent's competitive landscape is set to undergo major changes. The example of Kenya Airways is revealing. In just a few short years, the company's environment has changed radically. Nairobi has become one of Africa's three most served airports, with twenty-six carriers landing there. Some major European carriers are present there, as well as China Southern Airlines, but also Emirates which flies there three times a day, Qatar Airways four times a day, Etihad, Oman Air, Turkish Airlines, Rwandair, Ethiopian Airlines and South African Airways. "Ethiopian Airlines is in a similar situation. The Addis Ababa hub is also home to major European airlines, as well as Emirates, Etihad, Turkish and many others.

Aircraft manufacturers have taken note. Airbus expects an annual growth of 5% in the number of passengers on the continent[182] for a total of three hundred and three million in 2035. Consequently, it expects strong growth in the African market for new aircraft with a minimum capacity of one hundred seats. It predicts that the ten fastest growing domestic markets will be African[183] and estimates future orders at one thousand aircraft worth seventy-six billion dollars.

For the year 2017, Africa, with a 20.8% increase in air freight volume, is at the top of the ranking of the most dynamic zones in the field.[184] This spectacular increase can be explained in particular by the equally strong growth in trade between Africa and Asia.

South Africa, with which Ethiopia is associated, has been a partner in the aeronautics industry for thirty years and Tunisia has found a niche in the construction of small aircraft. For its part, Morocco has hosted the facilities of all the major players in the field, Airbus, Boeing, Bombardier and Embraer, joined by around a hundred operators in the sector. The kingdom has become a veritable continental hub, the African link in the global aeronautics chain. Beijing's strategists

---

182 Global growth is estimated at 4%, nearly 20% lower than it is expected in Africa.

183 Saul Butera, "Airbus sees Africa demand for 1000 jets over next 20 years", *Bloomberg Market*, February 24, 2017.

184 International Air Transport Association (IATA), 2017 Report.

have taken note. One of the fifteen agreements of 2016 between the kingdom and the middle empire was precisely about cooperation in the aeronautics sector.

Land mobility

With regard to land mobility, the needs are considerable as the investments of the previous century, colonial and post-colonial period were strictly limited. This extreme backwardness is one of the most costly obstacles to the economic development of the continent. Its effects make transport between capitals and regions, regions between them and countries between them hazardous. These effects have had and still have major consequences on interregional trade, the growth of which is indispensable for the development of the continent's markets and the reduction of imports, including agricultural imports.

The announced considerable increases in the number of vehicles and the volume of goods to be moved from one country to another make substantial investments indispensable. Slowly but surely, the countries of the continent are making a massive and indispensable correction to develop economic activity, increase the size of markets, increase the volume of trade, generate growth and wealth. Major works are multiplying in all parts of the continent. Tancé by its neighbour, Morocco leads with South Africa for the longest motorway network on the continent. In particular, the kingdom has built the trans-Saharan highway to Nouakchott and Rosso. Further south, from Mauritania to Nigeria, the trans-African coastal highway stretches over 3,775 km, or 83% of the major project, and crosses thirteen West African countries. In the East and in the Great Lakes region, numerous road construction projects are underway. Eventually, they will form a complete transport and communication network in these two major regions of the continent.[185]

Despite recent advances, the automotive market on the continent remains the most underdeveloped in the world. Indeed, the level of motorization is forty-four vehicles per thousand inhabitants compared to one hundred and seventy-six and eighty respectively for Latin America and South Asia. This situation gives rise to varying assessments. The assessment of Karthi Pillay, Deloitte's specialist on the African automotive market, seems to be the most widely accepted. "When Volkswagen and General Motors entered the Chinese market,

---

185 Eugene Berg, "The road from Cape to Cairo, from dream to reality in African Geopolitics", No 53-54, First Quarter, 2015.

it was even lower than the market in Ethiopia today. This fact did not prevent them from recognizing the long-term potential of the Chinese market."

Truth in China, truth in Africa? It seems so, with current and future prospects being favourable. Indeed, the automobile, truck and commercial vehicle sectors grew by 30% between 2005 and 2015 and are expected to grow by an average of 7.5% per year until 2025.[186]

Officials in the field have taken note. The South African analysis group B&B. has estimated that in 2025, ten million new vehicles will be sold on the continent compared to one million five hundred miles in 2015. This expected growth is due to an increase in the African middle class, which could reach half a billion by 2030; a supply of cheaper and better adapted new vehicles produced on the continent or from Europe and Asia; and stricter regulations in some countries concerning the dumping of used cars from Europe, the United States and Japan. According to Herbert Diess, Chairman of the Management Board of the Volkswagen brand, "Overall, car sales in Africa are expected to increase by 40% over the next five years. This is why we are expanding our activities there. »

Since Fiat, Ford, Mercedes and Toyota moved to South Africa in the 1960s and 1970s, and following the sanctions that undermined their operations in the country, the companies in the field have regained a foothold in Mandela's country, now in competition with Nigeria and the Kingdom of Morocco, which have also become major centres of a continuously growing continental production. In Morocco, automobile production is responsible for eighty-five thousand jobs and contributes to the country's exports to the tune of six billion dollars. In 2020, the volume of employment in the field could reach one hundred and seventy-five thousand jobs and its contribution to exports could reach ten billion dollars. Given the demand, it appears that there will be several hubs in automobile production in Africa, contrary to the wishes of the Abuja authorities who have worked to ensure that there is a single hub on the continent and that it is located in Nigeria?[187]

According to the specialist literature of the Mondor Intelligence consulting group, "in the Africa of the 2020s, the automobile industry will cease to be a luxury and become a necessity." In more restrained terms, Deloitte Africa shares this assessment. For economist Sarah

---

186 Mordor Intelligence, "Africa Automobile Market-Analysis of Growth, Trends Progress and Challenges (2017-2025)", Hyderabad, India, September 2017.

187 Price Waterhouse Cooper. Andrew S. Nevin, "Africa's Next Automotive Hub: reality Check", 2016.

Rundell, the development of this sector could even serve as a lever for the industrialization of the continent.

Nearly all the international production companies in the field have made the continent their home: Europeans, Americans, Asians, including Japanese, Koreans, Indians and Chinese. In addition, production tests are carried out on vehicles designed and produced on the continent.[188] This observation testifies to the attractiveness of the African market which, according to the analysis of Mordor Intelligence "offers great returns to players ready to invest".[189]

Toyota, the world's number one producer in the field is also number one in Africa. It controls 14% of the market there and has a presence in the fifty-four countries of the continent. Next come Renault and Hyundai with respectively 8% and 7.8% of the sub-Saharan market and the Korean Hyundai which, in 2016, exported one million vehicles to Africa.

The companies are investing prudently but are investing; the Americans in South Africa and Nigeria; the Europeans in Morocco, Tunisia, Nigeria, Kenya and Rwanda; the Japanese in South Africa and Nigeria; the Koreans in Morocco; the Chinese in Nigeria, Cameroon, South Africa, Algeria and Morocco;[190] the Indians in Ghana, Morocco and South Africa; the Iranians in Senegal. In view of the foreseeable demand, these companies will have to increase their investments for research, production and marketing of suitable products, their assembly and distribution, after-sales service and promotion of their brand because of the competition. According to McKinsey, "more than half of African households will have discretionary purchasing power by 2020. »

Companies will also have to accelerate their investments to meet the legitimate demands of governments and economic operators on the continent who will want to draw their share of the benefits of a growing market: share in research and technology transfer, share in jobs, economic and commercial activities, taxes, etc. Africa cannot be this growing automobile market and not see its participation in global motor vehicle production chains increase proportionally. This is partic-

188 Mobiva Motors in Kenya; Kantanka and Turtle in Ghana; Kiiramotors in Ouganda and Innoson in Nigeria.

189 Idem.

190 « Le constructeur chinois BYD va ouvrir une usine automobile au Maroc », *Les Echos*, December 11, 2017. The agreement provides for the installation of an assembly plant for electric cars, a plant for the construction of buses and trucks, and a third one for electric trains.

ularly the case in the Nigerian government's plan for the development of the automotive industry.[191]

It has been estimated that in 2015 only one third of the new vehicles sold on the continent are produced on the continent. If the status quo were to be maintained, this proportion would decline continuously and the situation would become untenable. The two million units produced on the continent are a mere fraction of the known and foreseeable private and public needs. The domain industry would normally be expected to fill this gap quickly. These are the objectives and ambitions of the African Automotive Industry Alliance (AAIA), which was established in 2015.

These goals and ambitions take various forms: Inclusion of the continent's facilities in global production and assembly lines; mutualization of distribution channels on the continent, such as the Indian holding company Tata-Africa and the Chinese company Automotive International Corporation from South Africa;production for specific markets, as the Indian group Mahindra and Mahindra with its sports vehicle production plant in Ghana are doing; penetration of the continental market, as the Peugeot group is doing from its facilities in Tunisia, the Renault and PSA groups from Morocco, and Volkswagen from its facilities in Ghana, Nigeria and Rwanda.

The ambitions are high. Fiat-Chrysler is pushing sales in 2017-18 with a growth target of 30%; the holding company Tata Africa (car distribution branch) aims to double its sales from five hundred million to one billion euros while the Renault group plans to sell one million units in 2020.

This progression is not without problems. In order to keep this field alive and well in Africa as in so many others, it is imperative that bank interest rates be kept at levels likely to support consumption, the increase in which has a direct effect on employment and growth. "Please, lower interest rates," exclaimed the President of Côte d'Ivoire in his speech in March 2018 at the Africa CEO Forum. That year, a bank loan for the purchase of a car on the continent fluctuated between 12% in Nigeria and 26% in Ghana, a rate unrelated to the rates charged in all other regions of the world. Beyond this question of interest rates, it is the offer of financial services that must be enriched and adapted to the vast markets of customers who will be, by hundreds of thousands, first-time buyers.

While the trade in used cars still meets undeniable needs at this stage, the volume, quality and age of vehicles are strictly regulated in

---

191 Automotive Industry Development Plan (NAIDP)

several countries. Indeed, this trade, which is very close to dumping, must not hinder the sustainable and profitable operations of the industry, including the setting up of vehicle production plants, the development of a real subcontracting sector, the sale of new cars, and financing formulas.

These developments in the automotive industry on the continent are also dependent on transport facilities, particularly maritime transport. Producing a car in Morocco and exporting it to the countries of the Gulf of Guinea is an operation that must be facilitated by the maritime routes and port facilities of the parties. Producing the same car in the south of the continent and having to ship it to these same Gulf countries via Amsterdam in the absence of maritime routes constitutes a suicidal operation.

The policy adopted by Nigeria could be adopted by national governments or economic communities on the continent, a policy linking the volume of vehicle imports to the volume of production in Africa of the same vehicles. Access to the market being linked proportionally to the establishment of industrial facilities.

Without a full opening of borders between the countries of the continent that produce motor vehicles and the countries that are not, and without demanding regulations on foreign motor vehicle manufacturing companies, it will be difficult to develop a large industrial automotive sector in Africa, given the development of the labour market and the financial, commercial and economic activity that it implies. In this case, as in so many others, the need to consolidate regional markets appears imperative.[192]

While in 2000, the Chinese market represented barely 1% of the world automobile market, its share rose to nearly 29% in 2017. In the same period, the US market share rose from 35% to 20%.[193] China is becoming the world leader in the automotive industry and will outstrip Europe and America, according to the director of the German Automotive Research Center. Also not to be forgotten is the lead taken by Chinese producers in the design and production of electric vehicles.

By supporting the development of this major sector, African countries will give their chance to the experiments underway on the continent for the production of electric vehicles such as those being tested in Africa by Kiira Motors and Ford.

---

192 « Les frontières à l'ère de la globalisation », *Problèmes économiques*, no 3112, Deuxième quinzaine, La Documentation française, 05,2015.

193 Julien Girault-Agence et Agence France-Presse. « La Chine en première place mondiale de l'industrie automobile », April 25, 2018.

Maritime mobility

For the first time in the contemporary period, the cluster of the world's maritime routes, of all the roads in the world, includes the multiple African relays. In 2011, seven hundred and five thousand containers from Europe were unloaded on the west coast of the continent against one million nine hundred and twenty-five miles from Asia. Since then, the number of these containers has been growing by nearly 8% per year. As a result of the considerable work that we will identify further, the total capacity of the major ports in West and Central Africa is gradually increasing from ten to twenty twenty-foot equivalent units. (TEUs) Their profitability should be in line with the continued growth in demand.

The slow growth of African exports was partly due to the dilapidated state of the continent's ports and the lack of connections between them and the continent's hinterland. The situation is evolving favourably. Investment in transport from country centres to ports and from one country to another or even from several countries to another is still too modest but nevertheless real. This investment alone is likely to produce the desired increase in production and exports.

The current developments involve much more than overtaking the maritime routes used almost exclusively for centuries between the continent and Europe to include those leading from the continent to Asia and the rest of the world. This normalization is another step in the decolonization of Africa. It illustrates the gradual integration of the continent into the world economy and its inclusion in the links that make it possible. Africans have yet to participate fully in this phase, which has been largely dominated by foreign interests that have invested substantially in the continent's port infrastructure in response to their own interests but also those of the African merchant class.

Initiatives are emerging to bridge this gap recognized by the Pan-African Association for Port Cooperation (PAPC), the continental federation of the three sub-regional port associations.[194] Created in 1999 with a view to creating a continental pool of expertise and sharing best practices, the APCP brings port authorities and the business community together at its biannual conference to discuss the challenges, issues and prospects of the sector.

These initiatives include the creation of a regional shipping company, Sealink, by the Economic Community of West African States

194 Ports Management Association of West and Central Africa (PMAWCA) – Port Management Association of Eastern and Southern Africa (PMAESA) and North African Port Management Association (NAPMA).

(ECOWAS) with the support of the African Development Bank (AfDB) and the Federation of West African Chambers of Commerce and Industry. The company will, among other things, ensure the transit of goods and passengers from West Africa in order to facilitate traffic and promote intra-African trade.

The history of maritime transport has been marked in recent years by a constant evolution towards the transport of ever-increasing volumes of goods reaching 10 billion tonnes in 2016; also towards ever-larger ships, exceeding five thousand container capacity and whose average size is twice that of the current fleet.[195] As a result, it is necessary to increase the depth of the basins to 16.5 metres, thus adjusting the capacity of ports to accommodate the new vessels and to handle goods using the most advanced logistical and technological systems.[196]

In targeted regions such as Africa, China is combining the modernization of existing port facilities or the construction of new deep-water ports with rail links to markets including its own. China has done so in Ethiopia, Kenya and South Africa. It is what European companies in the field have never done even when they had the initiative to do so. The saga of the railway to be rehabilitated and completed that runs from the port of Cotonou to Niger, Burkina Faso and finally Côte d'Ivoire is a perfect illustration of this sad situation.

It is said that the railway, including the TGV, has propelled a new China, brought about the emergence of new industrial poles, increased the mobility of goods and people, increased the volume of jobs and enriched the populations served. It had also made possible intra- and interregional trade, which brought growth and development. Between 2005 and 2025, China went from zero to 20,000 kilometres of high-speed rail, more than any other country in the world. These investments explain, at least in part, the country's tremendous economic progress. Why should it be any different in Africa?

Of course, China does not have a monopoly on these investments and major works. However, it is at the forefront of the forces that are redrawing the world's maritime map, including Africa, its coastal islands and inland territories. Colossal, these investments serve the interests of Chinese multinationals in the field, which operate nearly two-thirds of the world's container fleet. These Chinese multinationals - China Overseas Port Holding, China Ocean Shipping, China Mer-

---

195 « Les grands ports mondiaux », Questions internationales, La documentation française, no.70, November-December 2014.

196 « Review of Maritime Transport », United Nations Conference on Trade and Development, UNCTAD, 2015.

chants Group - live on the continent with the French groups Bolloré and CMA-CGM, the Danish Maersk, the Singaporean Nol and the Italian Mediterranean Shipping Company (MSC).

These investments in Africa and elsewhere in the world also respond to other needs of Chinese operators who, in 2016, ranked first in terms of maritime transport connectivity for containerised goods. Next come operators from Singapore, Hong Kong, the Republic of Korea, Malaysia and Germany. In this world, competition is fierce. Since the first version of this book was written, the two major Chinese companies have just merged and the Singaporean Nol has been bought by the French CMA CGM. The forces involved are constantly rethinking themselves.

The African continent has not remained on the sidelines of this strong evolution of the global maritime transport system. It has been estimated that 92% of goods, exports and imports combined, coming from or going to Africa depend on maritime transport. In line with the technological developments in this field, Africa has been experiencing, since the 2000s, an exponential growth in containerisation as a result, in particular, of renewed port management and the modernisation of the infrastructure in this field.

Cause or effect of a 7% annual growth in maritime traffic and a fourfold increase in trade volumes resulting from the growth of trade with Asia and China in particular, no less than fifty billion dollars have been invested in the African port sector between 2007 and 2017. In addition, there have been takeovers, such as the one that enabled the China Merchants Group to acquire, in 2010, 47.5% of the shares of the Lagos container terminal in Nigeria; 50% of the company responsible for the Lomé container terminal, 23.5% of the Djibouti terminal facilities facing the Strait of Bab-el Mandeb which separates the Horn of Africa and the Emirates peninsula, and 49% of the Terminal Link of the French group CMA CGM. As a result, the Chinese company has privileged access to the continent's international ports. Like the world's ports, which continue to grow richer as a result of the geopolitical changes taking place, the mapping of the continent's ports also shows a tremendous evolution.[197]

These vast changes have been largely initiated and deployed by China in accordance with a global strategy decided at the beginning of the century. This strategy aims to control land routes through Central Asia, sea routes through East Africa and the Suez Canal to finally

197 « Le secteur portuaire en Afrique: plein cap sur le développement », Proparco, no 26, April-May 2017.

reach Europe and, possibly, "ice" routes, the three passages that the melting ice pack will release in the Far North.

China, this historic maritime power is also a maritime power of the future with seven of the world's top ten ports, including Shanghai. Its strategy, which includes Africa, responds to an overall forecast that proved to be well-founded for this country, which in 2009 became the world's leading exporter and, by 2013, the world's leading trading power.

If China's exports of goods and services totalled two hundred and forty billion dollars in 2001, they will reach one thousand seven hundred billion in 2011 and 2480 billion in 2018. More than 80% of these exports go by sea. China has a clear interest in global maritime traffic.

Among these initiatives, it is also important to take the measure of the rapid and far-reaching transformation of almost all major ports on the mainland. This modernization provides Africa with the indispensable points of contact required to participate fully in the globalized economy.

On the shores of the Mediterranean, major ports have recently taken on a major dimension: Tangier Med in Morocco on the Strait of Gibraltar; Port Said, Damietta, Sokhane and Alexandria in Egypt, where huge works costing 2.5 billion dollars have transformed the Suez Canal into a wider and deeper passage. Inaugurated in August 2015, the new canal aims to strengthen its role as a key passage between Europe and Asia on one of the world's busiest shipping routes. Egypt expects traffic to double by 2023 and revenues to triple.[198]

On the Southern and Western Atlantic coasts, the movement is intense. Apart from the three ports of South Africa equipped with container terminals, the duo Durban-Cape Town, Port Elizabeth and Ngqura, the ports of Maputo are now to be counted on, which is experiencing spectacular growth, up by 17% in 2017 and offers with the ports of Beira and Nacala direct access to land, road and rail logistics corridors. Going up the coast, one can see the new deep-water port of Kribi in Cameroon, which is intended to complement the important port of Douala. In neighbouring Nigeria, the port of Lagos will lose its position as the country's leading port following the construction by the China Harbour Engineering Company (CHEC) of the continent's largest deep-water port in the Lekki Free Trade Zone. The price is high, at 1.6 billion dollars, but the expected benefits are considerable.

This excitement has also spread to the ports of Conakry, Sao Tome and Principe, Lomé, Cotonou upgraded and/or expanded. While in

---

198 « Le pari africain », *Jeune Afrique*, no 20917, December 4-7, 2016.

Ghana the port of Tema is being expanded, in Côte d'Ivoire a second terminal is being added to the port of Abidjan, both of which are capable of handling the world's largest container ships. Finally, in the South West of the country of Houphouët, the port of San Pedro is substantially enlarged.[199] DPWorld is the financier and prime contractor of the new port of N'Dayane in Senegal after having replaced the Boloré Group in 2007 as prime contractor for the modernization of the "port of the future" site and manager of these facilities until 2032.[200]

On the Red Sea coast, new ports have appeared largely financed by the United Arab Emirates, namely the ports of Doraleh, Berbera, and Massawa next to the ports of Tadjouraah and Goubet. Refurbished to the highest standards, the port of Djibouti, at the crossroads of the continent's maritime routes, the East and Europe, is the focus of all attention, from the Chinese, the Americans, the Emirates and the French, among others.

Lastly, on the coast of East Africa, the largest port in that region, the port of Dar es Salaam is currently undergoing major work to ensure its capacity to accommodate large container ships. Its capacity is expected to double from thirteen to twenty-five million tonnes as a result of a 9% annual growth in its activities over the last ten years. Tanzania is also at work in Bagamoyo. There it is completing the construction of a mega-port and an adjacent industrial zone connected to the Tanzanian rail network. In Mozambique, the ports of Maputo, Beira and Nacala offer their customers direct access to land, road and rail logistics corridors. Further south, Port Louis in Mauritius is targeting one million TEUs by 2025 and is modernizing accordingly.

At work is the China Harbour Engineering Company (CHEC), a subsidiary of the conglomerate China Communications Construction Co (CCCC), which is by far the main contractor for these major works and their financing and ultimately the manager of these facilities. Other major carriers are also at work, but much more modestly, including the Boloré, CMA CGM and MSC groups. Some major works, such as those at Kibri in Cameroon, were carried out by a Franco-Chinese consortium formed by the China Harbour Engineering Company and the Boloré Group. The port of Lomé is managed by a consortium formed by MSC and the Bolloré Group. Other partners are also involved, such as the Emirate Dubai Ports World (DPWorld), which obtained its first African concession in Djibouti and built the port of Doraleh next to the ports of Tadjouraah and Goubet. The pow-

199 Paul Tournet et Camille Valero, Prosarco, no 26, March-April 2017.

200 "Ports in the Horn", *The Economist*, July 21, 2017.

erful group has also set up a naval base in Assab, Eritrea, and the port of Somaliland.

These three areas of transport are and will be experiencing high levels of activity in the coming years. Completed or in progress, the work identified above fills historic gaps in the continent's economies: a lack of fluid and fruitful relations between major areas of the continent; and a lack of sustained links with all regions of the world. These relationships and linkages are essential for the growth of intra-African trade and the inclusion of Africa in the global economy.

An African space agency

In an important work,[201] Sékou Ouédraogo argues for a major pan-African initiative that could provide the continent with a space agency that federates and enriches the experiences conducted to date by South Africa, Nigeria, Egypt, Ethiopia, Ghana, Côte d'Ivoire, Gabon, Morocco and Algeria and, in this case, with the help of China, among others. The list could be expanded in the coming months with initiatives from Angola[202] and the Democratic Republic of the Congo.[203]

It is announced that a Nigerian will be sent into space by 2030. For its part, Ghana has had the Japanese space agency, JAXA, launch the first satellite entirely built by an African country. Regional organizations have been created, such as the Regional African Satellite Communications Organization (RASCOM), which has forty-five member countries and whose initiatives are decisive. Numerous companies have been created such as RascomStar-QAF, UkoWapi and Atepa Satellite Applications, a subsidiary of the Senegalese group Atepa.

Since 2010, the African Union has taken up the matter, set up a working group, adopted the African Space Policy and Strategy and decided to create a Pan-African Institute of Space Science located in South Africa and an African Space Agency domiciled in Egypt.[204]

This use of space meets undeniable needs: needs for analysis, control and exploration of the oceans, at least on the African side of the territorialization of the oceans, which is a major challenge for all

---

201 Sékou Ouéadrogo, « L'Agence spatiale africaine », Paris, l'Harmattan, 2015.

202 Emmanuel Atcha, « L'Angola lancera son premier satellite en décembre prochain », *La tribune Afrique*, October 13, 2017.

203 « Kinshasa: présentation de la maquette du premier satellite congolais », Radio Okapi, June 24, 2015

204 « Satellites: l'Afrique se tourne vers les étoiles », *Jeune Afrique*, no 2966, November 12-18, 2017.

the countries bordering the world. Thirty-eight of the continent's fifty-four countries have a coastline with the potential offered by the oceans, including the deep oceans: possible water supply, transport, security, communication, natural resources including minerals, fisheries, abyssal organisms and energy.

The United Nations Convention on the Law of the Sea, which entered into force almost a quarter of a century ago, determines the maritime zones belonging to national territories, including the exclusive economic zone which, in exceptional circumstances, may extend from 200 nautical miles to 350 nautical miles.[205] The seas that bring together 78% of the world's states are still "coveted spaces".[206] Bernadette Mérenne-Schoumaker's expression applies to Africa. The countries of the continent have difficulty controlling their marine territories, rights of passage and fishing activities. The work of the Institute of Space Science and the African Space Agency is likely to be able to assist in the control of African marine territories and activities.

Big pharma

The "Big Pharma" is also taking root on the continent, the "new Eldorado of pharmacy, after China and India.[207] "The drug market will total sixty billion euros in 2020, perhaps double that in 2040, or 15% of world consumption.[208]

Propelled by demographic growth, the gradual rise of a middle class and the increase in life expectancy, which is accompanied by numerous pathologies, the market is growing strongly, as are the establishments of major groups on the continent: China's Human well Healthcare in Mali; Fosum Pharma, which, by buying France's Tridem Pharma, is gaining a foothold in 30 countries; and Sansheng in Ethiopia, which, among others, is part of this strong movement that has gradually made Africa "the leading export market for the Chinese pharmaceutical industry. "The Indians, for their part, are currently established in the East and South of the continent: CIPLA in Uganda; Rambaxy, CIPLA and Dr. Reddy's in South Africa. Western women are widespread throughout the continent: Sanofi in Algeria, Morocco

205 « L'Atlas de l'eau et des océans », *Le Monde* – Hors série.

206 Bernadette Mérenne-Schoumaker, « Les mers sont toujours des espaces convoités », Idem, pp.100ss,

207 Chloé Hecketsweiler, « Les géants de la pharmacie misent sur l'Afrique », *Le Monde*, December 4, 2013.

208 Les enjeux pharmaceutiques dans le monde: l'Afrique. Le monde pharmaceutique. July 18, 2014.

and South Africa; Sandos in Cameroon; Cooper Pharma in Rwanda and Côte d'Ivoire; Aspen Pharmacare in South Africa; Novartis in Côte d'Ivoire, Nigeria, Algeria and Egypt; GSK in Kenya, Nigeria and South Africa.

Between 1975 and 1997, 1,233 new drugs were introduced to the world market, of which only 11 were for tropical diseases, six of which were for veterinary use.

The level and diversity of Asian and Western companies in the field show that the African drug market, which is growing at an annual rate of 10%, is gradually taking its place as a significant fragment of the world market. On the other hand, the balance between imports and production on the continent is far from satisfactory. The same observation applies to research. It seems that only a supply management policy at the level of the economic communities (ECOWAS), a policy that caps, for a time, the import levels of generic products can correct what needs to be corrected; accelerate the establishment of production units, incorporate the research needs specific to the continent and, collateral benefits, create good level jobs. There is growing pressure for the industry to not only distribute on the continent but to produce more. The Economic Commission for Africa is pushing for this. In February 2019, its Secretary-General, Vera Songwe, says that Africa "must stop exporting much-needed jobs to other continents and invest in its pharmaceutical industry to meet its needs and create jobs, of which it estimates 16 million. If by 2030, the Americas rank first in "business opportunities in the health sector," Africa ranks second. The Appeal is apparently heard if we are to believe the positions taken by African industrialists, including tycoon Aliko Dangote, who intends to explore, with his foundation, public-private partnership formulas and to invest in the field in conjunction with stakeholders.

Conclusion

The culmination of the changes mentioned in our introduction, the global shift in wealth and the universal roll-out of the digital age, is still to come. Their full effect belongs to the long duration of time. However, since the beginning of the century, their added value has engaged humanity in a new phase of its history which has gradually reached Africa.

What would Africa be today if the shift in wealth from West to East had not taken place and if China, India, Malaysia, Korea, Vietnam and other Asian countries had not had the capacity to invest in Africa and deploy their many and varied resources, financial, technological, logistical, entrepreneurial, etc.?

What would Africa be today without the deployment of the digital age that has opened up the continent in terms of information and communication and provided it, for the first time in history, with the full range of available technological tools in real time?

The digital age has not opened up the continent in a rhetorical mode closer to the desirable statistics so often declined in the past than to investment. It has enabled hundreds of millions of Africans to own, master and use the tools of this information and communication. The statement that in the near future Africans will form one of the largest communities of Internet users in the world, a community that could reach one billion by 2040, illustrates the power of what is happening and what has happened. Finally, the digital age has made it possible to put in place, across the continent, the services required for the use of these tools that provide access to universal knowledge. This use has already revolutionized the banking practices of Africans and is gradually reaching, on the continent as elsewhere in the world, agriculture, education, health, transport, security, governance and trade, etc., all of which have been affected by the digital age. It is the lever used by thousands of young Africans to create their jobs and businesses.

Combined, the shift in wealth and the deployment of the digital age have broken the geopolitical cadastre that greatly limited Africa's development and have given it access to globalization.

Africa's current and foreseeable advances, the convergence of which is creating a vision of the entire continent, are largely the result of these changes, which have the value of historical impulses. These changes have put an end to the Western monopoly on the production of science and technology, growth and development. They have served as a powerful lever for other regions of the world and have created in Asia and especially in China two compelling needs: the need for resources and the need for external markets.

Africa meets both of these needs. Together with Latin America, but more than Latin America, it has the natural resources that are indispensable for the continued growth of Asia, especially China. Moreover, all forecasts predict strong growth in demand on the continent and the consolidation of a market that has the potential to become one of the largest in the world. Asia, which has or has had similar experiences, has taken note. Thus, convergences of Asia-Africa interests have gradually developed, shedding light on the continent's current progress.

Several of these advances appear to be decisive.

In the first place, the Africa-Asia "linked destiny" marks a radical upheaval in the continent's relationship with the rest of the world. Indeed, without detaching itself from its historical relationship with the West, Africa has developed, in a short period of time, a vast and multifaceted link with the Asian powers. Gradually, the continent has become part of the South-South financial, economic and commercial circuits that are currently the most dynamic in the world. By all predictions, they will remain so as far as we can see in the future. The continent needs millions of jobs. It will not find them outside these channels, which, according to all projections, could total nearly one hundred and fifty trillion dollars in 2050 compared to fifty trillion dollars for the Atlantic area, fifty-eight trillion dollars for China compared to thirty-four trillion dollars for the United States.

The spectacular development of Africa's relations with Asia is one of the key events at the beginning of this millennium. In particular, it puts an end to the long dependence of the black continent on the Western zone and inaugurates an unprecedented relationship between Africa and the powers of the world that will want to integrate it into their strategies of assertion and the multiple networks that support these strategies. A “balance” that was apparently still sustainable yesterday has imploded and the political, economic, military and security consequences of this implosion will be felt over the long term.

This development of Africa-Asia relations has been materialized by colossal investments in transport and communication infrastructures, energy, the environment, agriculture and education. Colossal but still insufficient, these flows must be maintained and enriched. They are indispensable for the integration of the continent’s national economies into the regional economic communities and, eventually, into the continental free trade area.

This integration brings multiple growths: growth in production, employment, research, transport, consumption, trade, tax revenues for public investment.

This integration brings the continent’s economy closer to the global economy and global value chains. It bears the seeds of the continent’s economic victory which, together with the educational victory, will free Africans from the multiple limitations of history.

These are the consequences of the provision by Asian institutions of substantial financing, including patient capital, which Africa has so far always lacked; the consequences also of the provision of substantial technical resources for the upgrading or development of modern infrastructure, from railways to airports, from port facilities to national or transnational highways.

Also to be taken into account is the spirit of these completions, which removes the cumbersome conditionalities that, from principles to financial, legal and technical requirements, have ended up by diverting Western supply and perverting the relationship. The Asians are not without economic and geopolitical interests. However, the models applied in their relationship with the continent since the beginning of the century have undermined the norms and practices of Western cooperation, not to mention the volumes and conditions of accessible funding.

Another policy is being constructed, another policy based on principles of non-intervention that is in direct contradiction to the practices to which Africans have been subjected since independence. This is undoubtedly what Moussa Faki Mahamat, the Chairperson of the African Union Commission, had in mind when he described the China-Africa partnership as “unprecedented dynamism” in February 2019.

For some African thinkers, including Felwine Sarr, all these transfers from wherever they come from will have to be made “through societal models that we Africans will decide to put in place. Kersa for hospitality, Ngor for sense of honour, imihigo for commitment to the community, Paul Jouary lists some others, including 'ubuntu,' the old Zulu word that can be translated as "I am because we are," but also "terenga" for hospitality.[209]

The continent and Africans need results as quick, as spectacular, as extensive and as verifiable as those achieved by China in the last quarter of a century.[210] Nothing less. They are in a favourable negotiating position with their major Asian partners. The latter still needs its African presence as a lever for its sought-after preponderance in the world. It also needs it in order to have privileged access to the continent's market, which, by the middle of the century, will be one of the most important in the world.

As decisive as they are, and they are, these external stimuli alone do not explain the continent's current progress. Indeed, this progress would have been impossible without the active participation of Africans themselves, a participation that generates multiple creative convergences. We have enlightened them throughout this work.

These include public policies and administrators who have, in many countries, adjusted the legislative and regulatory conditions for economic development, including investment. According to the World Bank, one third of the reforms aimed at facilitating economic activity in the world have been carried out in Africa; to the governors and senior technicians who have identified and implemented the contents of the treaties creating regional communities, free trade areas to those that encompass the entire continent and are working for their effective deployment.

One thinks of the working groups of the public and private sectors which have imagined the new cities of the continent and the deployment of collective facilities better adapted to the needs of the time.

We are also thinking of the managers of financial institutions who are gradually regaining control of them through acquisitions and mergers; the managers of African insurance companies who are extending their prospecting throughout the continent; the managers of the continent's stock exchanges who, through the financial products offered, are raising the savings of Africans; the business leaders who are entering new markets at the national, regional, continental and international levels; the importers who have won the confidence of new partners in Asian markets.

---

209 Felwine Sarr, « L'Afrique n'est toujours pas décolonisée », *Jeune Afrique*, no 2878, March 6-12 2016.

210 Evan Osmos, « Chine l'âge des ambitions », Paris, Albin Michel, 2015.

Finally, African professional groups, including the business community, are making their voices and needs heard; African consulting firms and African think tanks are taking over from foreign firms and think tanks in defining the current and foreseeable needs of the continent. These contribute to the normalization and building of the Africa of tomorrow.

This standardization is incomplete, but it is under way and, as we have shown, it is unquestionably progressing. Many movements have resulted from this, and they constitute the real current events in Africa. Beyond these sectoral movements, this ongoing normalization is creating the conditions for a new inter-African dialogue on the needs of the continent and its populations, dialogue within and between intermediary bodies, dialogue within civil society and dialogue between civil society and governments. Something like the whole of Africa is gradually emerging, the totality of its interests and needs, its resources and powers.

For those who are attentive to events on the continent, this gradual reconfiguration of its energies is one of the strongest variations in progress from Cairo to Johannesburg. Eventually, it will not be the Asians who will replace the Europeans on the continent, but the Africans. From this totality will come governance adjustments responding to the needs of African societies, it being understood that politics rarely change societies, but that they often provoke political change.

As discussed throughout this book, there are many important and ongoing changes that require analysis, deliberation and decision by Africans.

These multiple changes feed off each other.

From a demographic enrichment imposing a doubling of the continent's population which, in 2050, will account for a quarter of humanity.

From a massively rural population to a population with an urban majority.

From an almost exclusive relationship with the former colonial powers to the development of relations with Asian powers, notably China, Africa's leading supplier of capital and trading partner.

From a totally fragmented economy limited by a territorial division of a colonial nature towards a slow but continuous regional integration, accelerated by the development of transport and communication infrastructures and the deployment of intra-continental financial, economic and commercial networks.

From a local market to a national and regional market which, together with that of India, could be the locomotive of the world economy in the long run of the century.

From a fragile scientific and technological position, to say the least, to a rapid and successful insertion into the digital age. By mid-century, the continent could contain one of the world's very first communities of Internet users. From a chronic communication gap to four hundred million Internet connections and more than six hundred million mobile phones.

Each of its crossings has known or will know exciting moments but also hollow moments, so great are the challenges to be met and the interests involved. However, these crossings are now a given and are undeniably unfolding in parallel and in convergence with each other. The time when Africans "imported their poverty and exported their wealth", in Aliko Dangote's words, the continent's first fortune, that time is fading.

One of the major consequences of this set of upheavals is the new capacity of Africans to choose their international partners; also to negotiate about what they offer the world and what they have a right to expect from it. No one today can speak for them or pretend to defend their interests. They now have multiple levers at their disposal to put an end to everything that sustains their dependence, to all the forms of dumping that undermine their momentum. Then they will be able to develop a supply management system that will serve their producers first and foremost in all material and immaterial fields. Africans can now demand that their international partners contribute to the wealth of the continent and its inhabitants by transforming the continent's resources on the continent, producing goods and services in Africa, joining forces with national groups, developing sub-contracting, practising technology transfers and making commitments relating to job creation, millions of jobs that African societies urgently need. Truth in Beijing, Sao Paulo, Warsaw, Mexico City...and in Yaoundé, Nairobi, Dakar and Abuja.

This book is based on the prediction that, in the 2020s and beyond, Africa's geopolitical weight will increase. The dominant powers, the United States on the one hand and China on the other, will seek its assistance in achieving the following three imperatives which they are pursuing and will continue to pursue: to consolidate their political preponderance and their military bases; to ensure the globalization of their infrastructures and clients, particularly digital ones[211]; and to benefit from access to one of the two exponentially growing markets, the African market. Finally, with regard to energy and environmental

---

211 "World War Web, The fight for the Internet's Future", *Foreign Affairs*, September-October 2018.

change, the contribution and participation of Africans is and will be imperative. They do not and will not have the choice of radicalism, as degradation is so decisive. If in 1960, Lake Chad occupied twenty-six thousand km2, fifty years later, in 2010, it only occupied one thousand five hundred km2. This restoration is imperative and so many others with it.

This positioning also concerns economic and commercial affairs, including, as a priority, the building and protection of African regional markets and policies of protection and supply management – for a time, at least – likely to consolidate these markets; including also production on the continent or the inclusion of companies on the continent in global production chains. As was the case for China, a real share of the new development of the continent must be entrusted to African enterprises operating independently or in partnership with foreign companies.[212] In the latter case, in addition to financial disbursements, the charges must include support for the development of endogenous research, the effective transfer of advanced technologies and the integration of a significant percentage of African managers and technicians in major works, from their design to their full implementation.

The African demographic dividend will serve as a basis for a more central positioning of the continent in world affairs, in the international institutions of the first century of the third millennium, new or radically renewed institutions. How can we put a quarter of humanity in brackets?

A new era of global governance is opening up, as it did in the aftermath of the Second World War. Of course, the geopolitical context has changed radically, as have the powers, and the list of issues and challenges has been enriched by new demands, imperatives and common interests. The countries of the world will have two options.

One can imagine an offer based on the extension of global governance as established in the 1950s. But this extension is made almost impossible by the shift in wealth and the universal deployment of the digital age.

Some point to another offer of global governance that is currently taking shape, in which China would be the clever protagonist. This offer that is under construction is rooted in the soil of the third millennium: the development of a second global financial, economic and commercial force, that of the old South combined with the new East; the establishment of new institutions whose purpose is to set common

---

212 « 500 premières entreprises africaines », *Jeune Afrique*, Hors série no 43, 2016.

standards and regulate international relations in the historical and digital space.

In the aftermath of the Second World War, Africa was, as it were, chained by the decisions of the colonial powers. It was "under civilizational and cultural injunction," and had nothing to say about the arrangements that prevailed then. Its situation is radically different today. A real and significant part of the reorganisation of current global governance or the new emerging governance must reflect its interests and needs: interests and needs that are its own and also those that it shares with the rest of the human family.

In this context, existing African continental institutions such as the African Union, the African Parliament, the Court of Justice and the African Development Bank are destined to become institutions of the highest importance on the planet as fiduciary and responsible (at least in part) for the overall interests of one in four people in the world; also for the expectations of a youth that is characterized "by a very different representation of space and narrative about their condition. They no longer agree with a discourse that is projected onto them, that no longer corresponds to the way they live in the world.[213] These continental institutions should normally be included in the short list of major poles of world affairs management in the 21st century.

Global, continental and national, the changes underway are not complete. However, they are setting the pace for the world and for the continent, a continent that was once marginalized and is now becoming, along with India, one of the great building sites of this century, perhaps even the greatest building site of this century.

Jean-Louis Roy

Montréal, March 29, 2019

213 Felwine Sarr, « Le Magazine de l'Afrique », 22 mai 2018.

Bibliography

Alexandre, L. (2018). La fin du monde? Pas tout de suite! *www.lexpresse.fr*. Consulté à l'adresse https://www.lexpress.fr/actualite/sciences/la-fin-du-monde-pas-tout-de-suite_1985099.html

Almeida-Topor, H. d'. (2010). *L'Afrique du XXe siècle à nos jours* (3e éd..). Paris: Armand Colin.

Anthony, You, Hug, Beise, Choi, Lee, Mshvidobadze, D. D. Y., Lucia Jan Yoonie Sinae Anastasia. (2017). *Generation 2030 Africa 2.0*. New York: UNICEF. Consulté à l'adresse https://data.unicef.org/resources/generation-2030-africa-2-0/

Assane Mayaki, I. (2018). Débats : l'identité virtuelle, une étape vers l'inclusion

Financière.*JeuneAfrique.com*.Consultéàl'adresse https://www.jeuneafrique.com/mag/578293/economie/debats-lidentite-virtuelle-une-etape-vers-linclusion-financiere/

Association Africaine desbourses de valeurs mobilières. (2015). *Les marchés financiers en Afrique : véritable outil de développement ?* (Rapport annuel 2015-2016 No. No 5). NEPAD-OCDE. Consulté à l'adresse https://issuu.com/objectif-developpment/docs/revuespd5_les_marches_financiers_en_afrique_fr

Baron, L. (2017). En Afrique, l'Internet gratuit grâce à Facebook, mais à quel prix ? *TV5MONDE*. Consulté à l'adresse https://information.tv5monde.com/afrique/en-afrique-l-internet-gratuit grace-facebook-mais-quel-prix-183114

Bello, A. S. (2017). *La régionalisation en Afrique: essai sur un processus d'intégration et de développement*. Paris: L'Harmattan.

Boukari-Yabara, A. (2016). Felwine Sarr. Afrotopia. *Afrique contemporaine, n° 257*(1), 150153. Consulté à l'adresse http://www.cairn.info/revue-afrique-contemporaine-2016-1-page-150.htm

Carrère d'Encausse, H. (2018). «Il ne faut pas juger le pouvoir autoritaire de Poutine à l'aune de nos seuls critères». Consulté à l'adresse http://www.lefigaro.fr/vox/monde/2018/03/16/31002-20180316ARTFIG00308-il-ne-faut-pas-juger-le-pouvoir-autoritaire-de-poutine-a-l-aune-de-nos-seuls-criteres.php

Cessou, S. (2015). Afrique: «l'émergence n'est ni un plan, ni un produit» [RFI]. Consulté à l'adresse http://www.rfi.fr/hebdo/20150515-afrique-emergence-pas-horizons-temporels-precis-alioune-sall-afrique-sud

C.L Nellor, D. (2008). David C. L. Nellor, Les marchés financiers en Afrique : véritable outil de développement, Finance et Développement, septembre 2008. – Recherche Google. Consulté à l'adresse https://www.google.com/search?q=David+C.+L.+Nellor%2C+Les+march%C3%A9s+financiers+en+Afrique+%3A+v%C3%A9ritable+outil+de+d%C3%A9veloppement%2C+Finance+et+D%C3%A9veloppement%2C+septembre+2008.&oq=David+C.+L.+Nellor%2C+Les+march%C3%A9s+financiers+en+Afrique+%3A+v%C3%A9ritable+outil+de+d%C3%A9veloppement%2C+Finance+et+D%C3%A9veloppement%2C+septembre+2008.&aqs=chrome..69i57.3038j0j4&sourceid=chrome&ie=UTF-8

Compaore, D. (2016). Marché boursier en Afrique : Entre ralentissement et second souffle. *ECODAFRIK.* Consulté à l'adresse http://www.ecodafrik.com/marche-boursier-en-afrique-entre-ralentissement-et-second-souffle/

Daziano, L. (2014). Pourquoi les Etats-Unis sont devancés par la Chine en Afrique.

FIGARO. Consulté à l'adresse http://www.lefigaro.fr/vox/economie/2014/08/08/31007-20140808ARTFIG00264-pourquoi-les-etats-unis-sont-devances-par-la-chine-en-afrique.php

Deloitte. (2015). La consommation en Afrique. Le marché du XXIe siècle. Consulté à l'adresse: https://www2.deloitte.com/content/dam/Deloitte/fpc/Documents/secteurs/consumer-business/deloitte_consommation-en-afrique_juin-2015.pdf

Deslandes, Su et Lamandé, J., Weltong, Juliette. (2015). Le soutien public à l'internationalisation des entreprises chinoises., (No 70), 47. Consulté à l'adresse https://cn.ambafrance.org/IMG/

pdf/bulletin_economique_chine_79_novembre_-_decembre-2.pdf

Elong-Mbassi, J.-P. (2018). Nous devons inventer un nouveau modèle, *Afrique Magazine*. Consulté à l'adresse https://www.afriquemagazine.com/jean-pierre-elong-mbassi-%C2%AB-nous-devons-inventer-un-nouveau-mod%C3%A8le-%C2%BB

Fal, G. (2018). Pour sortir du franc CFA, optons pour un Fonds monétaire africain. *JeuneAfrique.com*. Consulté à l'adresse https://www.jeuneafrique.com/mag/531882/economie/pour-sortir-du-franc-cfa-optons-pour-un-fonds-monetaire-africain/

Franco-Rwandaise, L. T. (2017). Discours du président ghanéen Nana Akufo recevant son homologue français Emmanuel Macron à Accra. Consulté 6 mars 2019, à l'adresse http://www.france-rwanda.info/2017/12/discours-du-president-ghaneen-nana-akufo-recevant-son-homologue-francais-emmanuel-macron-a-accra.html

Hugon, Sudrie, P., Olivier. (1999). *Bilan de la prospective africaine* (Recherche No. Volume 1) (p. 92). France, Paris: MINISTÈRE DES AFFAIRES ÉTRANGÈRES. Consulté à l'adresse https://wfsf.org/resources/leala-pedagogical-resources/reports-by-un-and-other-international-organisations/15-un-bilan-de-la-prospective-africaine1/file

Joël Té-Lessia, A. (2018). Assurances : Allianz passe à l'offensive pour combler son retard en Afrique. Consulté 6 mars 2019, à l'adresse https://www.jeuneafrique.com/mag/619274/economie/assurances-allianz-passe-a-loffensive-pour-combler-son-retard-en-afrique/

Kodjo-Grandvaux, S. (2016). Sénégal – Felwine Sarr : « L'Afrique n'est toujours pas décolonisée ». *Jeune Afrique. com*. Consulté à l'adresse https://www.jeuneafrique.com/mag/307679/culture/senegal-felwine-sarr-lafrique-nest-toujours-decolonisee/

Laurence, D. (2014). Pourquoi les Etats-Unis sont devancés par la Chine en Afrique. Consulté à l'adresse http://www.lefigaro.fr/vox/economie/2014/08/08/31007-20140808ARTFIG00264-pourquoi-les-etats-unis-sont-devances-par-la-chine-en-afrique.php

Le Bec, C. (2018). Commerce : comment Dubaï est devenu un tremplin pour l'Afrique ? Consulté 6 mars 2019, à l'adresse https://www.jeuneafrique.com/mag/543036/economie/commerce-comment-dubai-est-devenu-un-tremplin-pour-lafrique/

Lebras, H. (2017). 10 milliards d'humains, et alors ? Consulté à l'adresse https://www.lemonde.fr/idees/article/2017/12/07/10-milliards-d-humains-et-alors_5226163_3232.html

Leroueil, J. (2017). Venus d'ailleurs, ils ont fait fortune en Afrique. *Forbes Afrique*. Consulté à l'adresse https://forbesafrique.com/venus-dailleurs-ils-ont-fait-fortune-en-afrique/

Linge, I. (2019). L'Ethiopie sera en 2020 le premier pays, après la Suisse, à abriter le Forum Economique Mondial. *Agence Ecofin*, (No 67). Consulté à l'adresse https://www.agenceecofin.com/en-bref/2501-63513-l-ethiopie-sera-en-2020-le-premier-pays-apres-la-suisse-a-abriter-le-forum-economique-mondial

Maury, F. (2017). Banques : l'opportunité nationale. *JeuneAfrique.com*, (No 2970). Consulté à l'adresse https://www.jeuneafrique.com/mag/500849/economie/edito-banques-lopportunite-nationale/

Mbembé, J.-A. (2010). *Sortir de la grande nuit: essai sur l'Afrique décolonisée*. Paris: Découverte.

McGann, J. G. (2019). *2018 Global Go To Think Tank Index Report* (p. 266). University of Pennsylvannia. Consulté à l'adresse https://repository.upenn.edu/cgi/viewcontent.cgi?article=1017&context=think_tanks

Michel, L. (2015). Sommet Africités : 1,2 milliard d'urbains en 2050, le nouveau défi africain. *Franceinfo*. Consulté à l'adresse https://www.francetvinfo.fr/monde/afrique/afrique-du-sud/sommet-africites-1-2-milliard-d-urbains-en-2050-le-nouveau-defi-africain_3064797.html

Moscovici, P. (2016). *S'il est minuit en Europe* (Grasset). Paris: Bernard Grasset.

Nubukpo, K. éditeur intellectuel, Ze Belinga, M., Tinel, B., & Dembélé, D. M. (2016). *Sortir l'Afrique de la servitude monétaire: à qui profite le franc CFA?* Paris: La Dispute.

OCDE. (2010). *Perspectives de développement mondial 2010 : le basculement de la richesse. Paris, OCDE, 2010. - Recherche Google*. Paris: OCDE. Consulté à l'adresse https://doi.org/10.1787/9789264084742-fr.

Pachauri, R. K. (2015). *Changements climatiques 2014: rapport de synthèse : contribution des Groupes de travail I, II et III au cinquième Rapport d'évaluation du Groupe d'experts intergouvernemental sur l'évolution du climat*. Genève (Suisse): GIEC.

Rédaction. (2018). Entretien exclusif avec S.E Hamad Buamim, Président de la Chambre de Commerce de Dubaï. Consulté 6 mars 2019, à l'adresse https://www.financialafrik.com/2018/09/07/entretien-exclusif-avec-s-e-hamad-buamim-president-de-la-chambre-de-commerce-de-dubai/

Rifai, T. (2017). Les forteresses touristiques ne sont pas la meilleure stratégie. *Jeune Afrique*, (2947).

Roy, J.-L. (2014). *Bienvenue dans le siècle de la diversité: la nouvelle carte culturelle du monde*. Montréal: Stanké.

Santi, M. (2019). Franc CFA, clé de voûte de la Françafrique. Consulté à l'adresse https://www.latribune.fr/opinions/tribunes/franc-cfa-cle-de-voute-de-la-francafrique-807222.html

Scott, S. (2010). Quels sont les déterminants du développement des marchés financiers d'Afrique subsaharienne. Consulté 6 mars 2019, à l'adresse https://blog.secteur-prive-developpement.fr/2010/04/22/les-determinants-du-developpement-des-marches-financiers/

Sévérino, J.-M. (2016). *Entreprenante Afrique*. Paris: Odile Jacob.

Smith, S. (2018). *La ruée vers l'Europe: la jeune Afrique en route vers le Vieux Continent* (Grasset). Paris: Bernard Grasset.

Taillefer, G. (2017). Réussir la transition. *Le Devoir*. Consulté à l'adresse https://www.ledevoir.com/opinion/editoriaux/505621/afrique-reussir-la-transition

Tchemedie, J. (2019). Afrique : Selon la GSMA, les technologies mobiles contribuent à 7,1% au PIB. Consulté 6 mars 2019, à l'adresse https://www.digitalbusiness.africa/afrique-selon-la-gsma-les-technologies-mobiles-contribuent-a-71-au-pib/

UNICEF. (2014). *Afrique, génération 2030. De 1,2 à 2,4 milliards de personnes.* UNICEF. Consulté à l'adresse https://www.unicef.org/french/publications/files/UNICEF_Africa_Generation_2030_fr.pdf

UNICEF. (2017). *Generation 2030, Africa 2.0, UNICEF,*. Consulté à l'adresse https://data.unicef.org/wp-content/uploads/2017/10/Generation_2030_Africa_2.0_Executive_Summary_25Oct17_FRENCH.pdf

UNION AFRICAINE. (2012). *"INTENSIFICATION DU COMMERCE INTRA-AFRICAIN" Questions liées au commerce intra-africain, Plan d'action proposé pour l'intensification du commerce intra-africain, cadre pour l'accélération de la mise en place d'une Zone de libre-échange continentale.* Addis Ababa. Consulté à l'adresse https://www.google.com/search?ei=TR1_XNH2IaXQjwSShp6QDw&q=Union+africaine%2C+Intensification+du+commerce+intra-africain%2C+Conf%C3%A9rence+de+l%E2%80%99Union+africaine%2C+29-30+janvier+2012.+%2F+&oq=Union+africaine%2C+Intensification+du+commerce+intra-africain%2C+Conf%C3%A9rence+de+l%E2%80%99Union+africaine%2C+29-30+janvier+2012.+-

%2F+&gs_l=psy-ab.3...22098.25019..25180...0.0..0.8.15.2......0....1j2..gws-wiz.....0.3B3pvjjqj6s

Walid Kefi. (2018). Pour l'Inde, se rapprocher de l'Afrique devient une affaire d'Etat. *africaleadnews*. Consulté à l'adresse http://africaleadnews.com/pour-linde-se-rapprocher-de-lafrique-devient-une-affaire-detat/

Xiaoyang, T. (2014). Investissements chinois dans l'industrie textile tanzanienne et zambienne: De l'aide au marché. *Afrique contemporaine*, (250), 119132. Consulté à l'adresse https://dialnet.unirioja.es/servlet/articulo?codigo=6030824

Yacouba Barma, A. (2017). Chine-Afrique : un partenariat largement sous-estimé selon McKinsey. Consulté à l'adresse https://afrique.latribune.fr/finances/investissement/2017-06-28/chine-afrique-un-partenariat-largement-sous-estime-selon-mckinsey-742099.html

Yonga, R. (2014). Guide des Fonds Souverains africains. African Markets. Consulté à l'adresse https://www.google.ca/search?ei=0Cd_XNyLEtKK5wKIyZzgCw&q=R.+Yonga%2C+Guide+des+Fonds+Souverains+africains+%E2%80%94+African+Markets&oq=R.+Yonga%2C+-Guide+des+Fonds+Souverains+africains+%E2%80%94+African+Markets&gs_l=psy-ab.3...147186.150210..150534...0.0..0.202.207.1j0j1......0....1j2..gws-wiz.....0._8KdyncQgbo

Zyad, L. (2018). Ismaïl Omar Guelleh : «Djibouti est libre de ses choix ! », *377*. Consulté à l'adresse https://www.afriquemagazine.com/isma%C3%AFl-omar-guelleh-%C2%ABdjibouti-est-libre-de-ses-choix-%C2%BB